Jesus Unmasked

The Truth Will Shock You

Todd Friel

What others are saying about *Jesus Unmasked* . . .

A highly-readable book about the most important person ever — Jesus the Christ.

— David Wheaton
author and host, *The Christian Worldview*

Jesus Unmasked will blast a bright light into a dark and dying world. Give *Jesus Unmasked* to the atheist in your life.

— Ray Comfort

I love the wit and freshness of Todd Friel's teaching, and how he doesn't flinch in the face of hard truths. His love of Scripture and passion for sound doctrine always come through — even when he is wisecracking. But he is at his very best when explaining thorny but important theological questions. That's why I'm so excited about this book. No matter where you are in the Christian walk, you'll find *Jesus Unmasked* a profitable and spiritually uplifting study.

— Phil Johnson

Jesus Unmasked will silence any Bible critic.

— Ken Ham
Answers in Genesis

Todd Friel has written the book you always wanted to give to your friends. *Jesus Unmasked* is clear, direct, and simple, all without ever being shallow. Get several copies so you can share them with friends who need Jesus.

— Tedd Tripp
author and conference speaker

About the Author

Todd Friel is the host of *Wretched Radio*, a daily syndicated talk radio program, as well as host of *Wretched TV*. *Wretched Radio* is heard on 200 stations nationwide and *Wretched TV* is available in over 100 million households. Todd is the husband of one wife and father of three children.

Website: www.wretchedradio.com

Twitter: www.twitter.com/Wretchedradio

Facebook: facebook.com/wretchednetwork

First printing: August 2014
Second printing: November 2014

New Leaf Press, P.O. Box 726, Green Forest, AR 72638

New Leaf Press is a division of the New Leaf Publishing Group, Inc.

ISBN: 978-0-89221-726-7
Library of Congress Number: 2014945607

Cover by Diana Bogardus

Author's note: The Bible was not originally written on a computer. The inspired writers of the Bible had neither emoticons, italics, nor bold lettering. As you read the Bible verses contained in this book, I have bolded them to highlight a word or thought. Do not expect to see these in bold in your Bible.

Please consider requesting that a copy of this volume be purchased by your local library system.

Printed in the United States of America

Please visit our website for other great titles:
www.newleafpress.net

For information regarding author interviews,
please contact the publicity department at (870) 438-5288

New Leaf Press
A Division of New Leaf Publishing Group
www.newleafpress.net

Thank you

Proverbs 31:10 asks, "An excellent wife, who can find? For her worth is far above jewels." Well, I found one.

It is not uncommon for someone to meet my wife and inform me, "You married above your pay grade." Indeed. This book would not have been possible without Susan. She let me spend Christmas vacation writing this. I didn't even have to put up decorations. That is a good wife.

It was my wife who introduced me to the fascinating study of types and shadows years ago. She took a Kay Arthur Inductive Bible Study on the Book of Hebrews where she learned much about the Old Testament tabernacle and the rich imagery of covenants. I owe her, and Kay Arthur, many thanks for the chapters on the tabernacle and covenant. If you are in search of a great women's Bible study, you can't do better than Kay Arthur.

Thank you, Sweetheart. I mean my wife, not Kay Arthur.

Thank you to my wonderful daughters for volunteering to proofread Dad's work and offering their very helpful feedback. They didn't even charge me.

Okay, I lied, they didn't volunteer. I duct-taped them to a chair and forced them to read this. But they are still great kids and I love them to pieces.

I would also like to thank Starbucks for all of the electricity they gave to me with their overpriced but supposedly environmentally friendly coffee while I typed away. Oh, and thanks for the attitude.

Thanks to Ray Comfort for having the aggressive idea to travel to 13 European countries in 13 days for the *Way of the Master* TV show. Ray assigned me the task of visiting monuments of the great Protestant reformers. I left for Europe with a profound commitment to truth. I returned from Europe with a burning passion to defend that truth.

Our Protestant forefathers were strangled, quartered, and burned for the truth. Thanks to Ray, I am willing to do the same.

Additionally, thank you to all of my teachers throughout the years who lived for the truth. This entire book is a compilation of what I have learned from godly men who dedicated their lives that others would have "the faith which was once for all handed down to the saints" (Jude 3).

Thanks also to Tim Dudley for flying to Atlanta to enlist me to the New Leaf team. It is a joy to work with the entire pile of leaves.

Finally and firstly, thank You to my Savior. Thank You for rekindling my heart as I wrote this. May You use it so others might know You, the Truth.

Contents

Introduction: Truth Is Like a Baseball Game 9

Chapter 1: Who Is This Man? 17

Chapter 2: The Big Question 21

Chapter 3: Big, Fancy Words 27

Chapter 4: The Scarlet Thread in the Old Testament 33

Chapter 5: The Scarlet Thread in the New Testament 41

Chapter 6: Jesus Is the Ark 51

Chapter 7: Jesus Is the Rock 65

Chapter 8: Jesus Is the Living Water 73

Chapter 9: Jesus Is the Bread 79

Chapter 10: Jesus Is the Bronze Serpent 85

Chapter 11: Jesus Is the Tabernacle 93

Chapter 12: Read This! 107

Chapter 13: Jesus Is the Sabbath 115

Chapter 14: Jesus Is Seven Festivals 129

Chapter 15: The Offices of Jesus 143

Chapter 16: Jesus Is People 161

Chapter 17: Jesus Is Places and Things 175

Chapter 18: Jesus Is the New Covenant, Part One 183

Chapter 19: Jesus Is the New Covenant, Part Two 201

Chapter 20: Jesus Is the I AM 215

Chapter 21: Jesus Is the Bridegroom 223

Chapter 22: Jesus Is 233

Scripture Reference Guide 236

Truth Is Like a Baseball Game

From approximately A.D. 33 until approximately A.D. 1400, a baseball umpire would call 'em as they are.

From approximately A.D. 1400 until approximately 1989, a baseball umpire would call 'em as he sees them.

From approximately 1989 until today, a baseball umpire would call them and that is what they are.

Notice the difference?

Pre-modernism: Approximately A.D. 33 until Approximately 1400

During the pre-modern era, Western civilization generally acknowledged the existence of a divine being as revealed in the Bible. Pre-modern people accepted the teachings of the Church and Scripture with little skepticism. "God said it, that settles it."

But something changed. Around the 1400s, skeptics began to question the existence of God and the truthfulness of the Holy Bible. Philosophers from Machiavelli to Voltaire paved the way for society to question the authority of the Scriptures.

The Protestant Reformation contributed to this new way of thinking. As reformers questioned and defied the authority of the Roman Catholic Church, laypeople began to believe they could do the same. This ushered in the modern era of empiricism. Man and science became the supreme authorities while God and the Church began to take a back seat.

The Modern Era: Approximately 1400 until Approximately 1989

As the centuries marched along and technology advanced (especially during the late 19th-century industrial revolution), man was feeling rather confident that he alone possessed the truth. The modern era between 1400 and 1989 was the heyday of man. Empiricism and science were the kings of truth. Unfortunately, four W's showed up and wrecked everything.

World War I was the bloodiest conflict in human history. Unfortunately, what was supposed to be the "war to end all wars" was just a warm-up for the greatest blood bath ever: World War II. Suddenly mans' confidence in man was rocked. If we are supposed to know the answers to everything, why is the world so dangerous and unstable? Man's skepticism of man had begun.

Postmodernism: Approximately 1989 until Today

By the end of the 20th century, culture concluded that humans are not the repositories of truth we once imagined. When the Berlin Wall came tumbling down in 1989, man made a decision, "We don't know what truth is."

Talk about a conundrum. If man doesn't know the truth and the Bible doesn't know the truth, then who does? Answer: nobody and everybody. We are all right and nobody is wrong. Truth is no longer objective but subjective. Welcome to the post-modern world.

Our present postmodern age sounds like this:

> I don't agree with you, but I don't believe you are wrong.
> As long as it works for you, then it is true.
> Even though we completely disagree, we are both right.
> Truth is out, truthy is in.

A Bench Is a Watermelon

Several years ago I visited a seminary. I don't want to name names, so let's just say the school is called Columbia Theological Seminary in Atlanta, Georgia. I struck up a conversation with a fellow who was studying for his master's degree in theology. I sensed he was a postmodern.

"Sir," I asked while pointing at a bench, "what is that?"

He replied, "It is a bench."

"I think it is a watermelon. Am I wrong?"

The fellow replied quite naturally, "No, you are not wrong."

Two Plus Two Equals Whatever

Again, not to name names, let's just say I was at Georgia Tech talking to a young man. I smelled postmodernism.

"What is two plus two?" I asked.

"Four."

"I think it is seven. Am I wrong?"

"No."

"Then you think I am right?"

"No."

"Then you think I am wrong?"

"No."

"Then you think I am right?

"No."

Here comes the punch line: this fellow was studying to become an engineer. Remind me to never drive over one of his bridges.

Truth vs. Preferences

Truth is definitive. Preferences are not.

Truth is factual. Preferences are opinions.

Truth is provable. Preferences cannot be tested.

Quiz Time

True or false? Cleveland is in Ohio.

True or false? John Kennedy was assassinated.

True or false? John Kennedy had the best hair of any president.

True or false? Elvis wore increasingly tight white jumpsuits.

True or false? Elvis was the best singer ever.

True or false? Penicillin unplugs your drain.

True or false? Penicillin fights bacteria.

True or false? Monet painted in the impressionist style.

True or false? Monet is a better painter than Degas.

You see, some things are factual while other things are preferential. Some things can be proven through scientific methods or observation, while other things simply are not provable. Things that are not provable are merely preferences.

Is coffee made from coffee beans? Absolutely.

Does coffee taste good? It depends on who is drinking it.

Truth can be tested and verified because truth will always be true. Truth does not change. Truth is always the same, but not all things can be proven.

What about Religion?

Postmoderns are quick to say, "Your religion is true if it works for you."

Umm, no it's not. Just because something "works" does not mean it is true. A convicted criminal on death row can get through the day believing he is going to be released tomorrow, but his belief is misplaced; his faith is wrong. It may "work," but it is not correct.

Many cultists believe that their faith has helped them, and perhaps it has, but that does not mean a belief in Zeus or a carved idol is correct.

If I believe that Oprah Winfrey is the goddess of the universe, like millions do, and I will spend eternity with her in a Chicago high-rise if I read each of her magazines cover to cover and say, "Stedman is groovy" three times, will I be spending eternity in the Windy City on the 50th floor with O? Of course not, I would be wrong.

Let's say that I really, really, really believed that. Would the intensity of my belief send me to eternity with Oprah? Nope. Intensity of faith does not make it so.

What if a lot of people believed the same thing? What if there were a billion Oprah-ites? Would we all spend forever with Ms. Winfrey? Nein. Majority vote doesn't make something right.

Can you prefer one religion over another? Yes, you can; you can prefer anything you want. You can like one thing more than another, but that does not make the object of your affection true.

> You can prefer that 4 times 4 is 24, but you are wrong.
> You can prefer injecting a shot of Drano to cure lockjaw, but you are wrong.
> You can prefer plugging your computer into the cat, but you are wrong.

You can prefer being any religion you choose, but your preference does not make it true. You can prefer being a Christian, Buddhist, Hindu, Muslim, or Mormon, but that does not make your religion correct. Faith can be misplaced.

So how do we know what religion, if any, is actually true? We must examine their claims and determine if they are true or not. Can that be done? Absolutely.

Truth Is Not an Opinion

Two thousand years ago, a Roman governor dismissively asked Jesus Christ, "What is truth?" Unfortunately, Pontius Pilate did not ask that question with a genuine desire to hear the answer. Had he waited for a response, he would likely have heard what Jesus often claimed about Himself, "I am the way, and **the truth**, and the life" (John 14:6).

For centuries, the Western world accepted His answer, but recently skeptics and liberal theologians have disagreed with Jesus. Many have offered a different understanding of Jesus ranging from a good teacher to a figment of mans' imagination. Many have sought to put a mask on Jesus of Nazareth.

Why Bother?

Why should you take the time to encounter the real Jesus Christ?

> - He changed the calendar from B.C. to A.D., He must be kind of important.
> - He has more followers than the Rolling Stones, Beatles, and Miley Cyrus combined.
> - He claimed that He will personally sentence you to a room with a view on the lake of fire if you fail to believe in Him. A pretty serious accusation.

No other religious leader besides Jesus Christ makes exclusive claims on the truth. No other guru claims that his system is correct and you better believe it or you will suffer eternal consequences. The biblical Jesus does.

Let's Make a Deal

If you take the time to read this book, you will learn:

> - What Jesus believed about Himself
> - Why Jesus' contemporaries wanted to murder this "good teacher"

> What the Bible is actually about. It will make sense, whether
> you believe it or not.

If you take the time to read this book, you can draw your own conclusions about the most influential man in history. You can determine if Jesus is merely a role model or the Redeemer. You can determine if Jesus is a myth or the Messiah. You can determine if Jesus is *a* way or *the* way.

Prepare to see the unmasked Jesus and discover who this man really is.

250	●
	⊶ A.D. 33: Jesus crucified
	⊶ A.D. 30: Jesus begins ministry
	⊶ A.D. 26: John the Baptist begins preaching
0	◉ ⊶ 0: Jesus is born
	⊶ 397–5 B.C.: The silent years
250	●
	⊶ 397 B.C.: Malachi is Israel's last prophet until John the Baptist
500	● ⊶ 515 B.C.: Jerusalem rebuilt and temple completed
	⊶ 536 B.C.: Jews start returning to Jerusalem
	⊶ 586 B.C.: Southern Kingdom falls to Babylon
750	● ⊶ 721 B.C.: Northern Kingdom falls to Assyria
	⊶ 975 B.C.: Israel split in two
1000	◉ ⊶ 1004 B.C.: Solomon's temple completed
	⊶ 1015 B.C.: Solomon becomes king
	⊶ 1055 B.C.: David becomes king
1250	●
	⊶ 1451 B.C.: The Jews enter the Promised Land
	⊶ 1491–1451 B.C.: The Jews wander the desert
1500	● ⊶ 1491 B.C.: Moses leads the Exodus out of Egypt
	⊶ 1700–1574 B.C.: Joseph and his brothers have lots of babies
	⊶ 1739 B.C.: Joseph sold into slavery in Egypt
1750	●
	⊶ 1836 B.C.: Jacob born
	⊶ 1896 B.C.: Isaac born
2000	● ⊶ 1996 B.C. Abraham born
2250	●
	⊶ 2349 B.C.: Noah and the Global Flood
2500	●
2750	●
3000	●
3250	●
3500	●
3750	●
4000	●
	⊶ 4004 B.C.: Creation, Adam and Eve, Cain and Abel

Timeline
4004 B.C. – A.D. 33

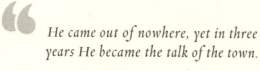

He came out of nowhere, yet in three
years He became the talk of the town.

Chapter One

Who Is This Man?

The city was buzzing. This was not the eager anticipation of an upcoming special event attended by a few ticket holders. This was the electricity that comes from a tragedy that affects everyone in the country. Think Kennedy assassination. Think 9/11. Think stock market crash of 2007.

Jesus Christ was dead. Everyone in Jerusalem knew He had been horrifically beaten and executed. They witnessed the trial with their own eyes and saw Him writhing on a Cross. Eyewitnesses watched Him die.

His naked body was removed from the Cross and placed in a tomb, but three days later His corpse was missing. Rumors raged. There was only one conversation that preoccupied everyone in Jerusalem, "Where is the body of Jesus the Christ?"

The Most Famous Man in Israel

Jesus of Nazareth was undeniably the most famous man of His day. If there had been gossip tabloids in A.D. 33, pictures of Jesus Christ would have been splattered on every cover.

> > There He goes again!
> > Jesus rebukes the Pharisees. To their faces!
> > No more sick people in Israel. What will Jesus do now?
> > Jesus Christ receives death threats.

He came out of nowhere, yet in three years He became the talk of the town. Why? What made Jesus the most popular man in Israel?

Illnesses Obliterated

Imagine a man who could heal people. Not a flaky televangelist charlatan, but an actual miracle worker. Now imagine this man traveled throughout the country healing every single sick person who was brought to Him.

Hospitals would be emptied. Handicap parking signs would be removed. Your loved one would be restored to complete and total health.

That was Jesus, the miracle worker from Galilee who healed those with faith or without faith. He healed everyone. Totally. Freely. Instantaneously.

> While the sun was setting, **all those** who had any who were sick with various diseases brought them to Him; and laying His hands on **each one of them**, He was **healing them** (Luke 4:40).

During the three years of Jesus' ministry, illness was effectively wiped out in Israel. No blindness. No deafness. No cancer. No kidney disease. No intellectual disability. No shingles. No blocked arteries. No muscular dystrophy. No Parkinson's disease. No cerebral palsy.

Gone. All disease was obliterated.

If you or a family member had not been healed by Jesus, you certainly knew someone who had. Nobody's life was unaffected by Jesus Christ. Everyone in Israel wanted to know, "Who exactly is this man?"

What He Taught

Not only was Jesus a genuine miracle worker, He was a teacher who said things that shocked those who came to hear Him preach. Jesus said things that were scandalous.

Here is the scene: Jesus was in a house teaching as crowds from all over Israel gathered. The home was filled to capacity. In the meantime, friends of a paralyzed man carried their crippled friend on a mat to place him in front of Jesus in hopes that He would heal their loved one. As they approached the house, the crowds were so thick they couldn't get to the man who was the focus of everyone's attention. Another plan was required.

The friends climbed to the roof of the home, removed the shingles and lowered their paralyzed friend on his mat in front of Jesus. What Jesus said next was scandalous. "Friend, your sins are forgiven you" (Luke 5:20).

Only God can forgive sins. Who did this man think He was? God?

How He Taught

Jesus said and did things that were shocking, but He also spoke and behaved in a way that was different than other preachers and teachers.

> When Jesus had finished these words, the **crowds were amazed** at His teaching; for He was teaching them as **one having authority**, and not as their scribes (Matt. 7:28–29).

When little children were brought to Him for a blessing, Jesus sat them on His knee. This was not the behavior of the other religious leaders in Israel. The Pharisees and Sadducees wore splendid robes and would never stoop to hug children and babies. Jesus did. Who is this man?

The Last Week of His Life

After three years of preaching, teaching, and healing, Jesus entered the city of Jerusalem on Monday to celebrate the Passover. Without a single tweet, the entire city knew Jesus was coming to town.

Throngs gathered as Jesus entered the city on a donkey. Hundreds of thousands of people lined the streets and spread their coats on the road as an act of homage. Palm branches were cut from trees and placed at the feet of the donkey.

> When He had entered Jerusalem, **all the city** was stirred, saying, **"Who is this?"** (Matt. 21:10).

Just four days later, the same crowds who gathered to welcome Him with chants of "Hosanna" gathered in front of Roman governor, Pontius Pilate, chanting, "Crucify Him. Crucify Him." Pilate honored their request and had Jesus whipped, mangled, and crucified. The man who entered Jerusalem triumphantly on Monday was disfigured and dead on Friday.

Three Days Later

On Sunday morning, rumors were swirling. The body of Jesus was missing from His tomb. What happened to Him? Was His body stolen? Who did it? Was His death a hoax? Did He rise from the dead the way He had raised others?

The city was buzzing, "Who is this man?"

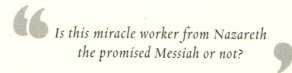
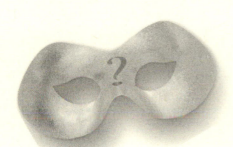

Chapter Two

The Big Question

How could adoring fans go from chanting, "Hosanna in the highest" to "Crucify Him" in a matter of days? How could one man move people from praising Him to petitioning His death sentence in the course of 96 hours?

The pendulum swung based on one question, "Who is this man?"

Jesus' Last Name Is Not Christ

Christ is His title. It means "anointed one" or "messiah." The question that swung the pendulum from adoration to rage was, "Is Jesus the Christ?"

The Old Testament had prophesied a messiah for centuries and the Jewish people had been anxiously waiting for the fulfillment of these promises. Most anticipated a political leader who would overthrow the oppressive Romans, but Jesus rejected their advances to make Him an earthly king. He was after something bigger, something spiritual and eternal.

Despite His crystal clear preaching and all of the miracles that Jesus performed, the Jews were confused. If Jesus is the fulfillment of all of the Old

Testament prophecies, why doesn't He act like a military general or political deliverer? Is this miracle worker from Nazareth the promised Messiah or not?

Question #1

When Jesus was arrested, thanks to Judas Iscariot, He was brought before the high priest of Israel for trial. False witnesses were called while Jesus remained silent. Finally, the high priest asked Him the million-shekel question, "Are You the Christ?" (Mark 14:61).

When Jesus answered, "I am," the high priest tore his clothes (an old-fashioned way of saying, "I am not happy") and condemned Him to death. Lacking the power to carry out the execution, the religious leaders sent Jesus to the Roman governor for a second trial.

Question #2

As the Jewish leaders presented their case to Pontius Pilate, they altered their accusation against Jesus to make it less religious and more secular, "We found this man misleading our nation and forbidding to pay taxes to Caesar, and saying that He Himself is Christ, a King."

So Pilate asked Him, saying, "Are you the King of the Jews?"

And He answered him and said, "It is as you say" (Luke 23:2–3).

Question #3

As Jesus was hanging on His Cross between two criminals, one of them mocked, "Are You not the Christ? Save Yourself and us!" (Luke 23:39). Even the criminals knew the tabloid headline, "Is Jesus the Messiah?"

How Could They Blow It?

Even Jesus' disciples were confused when He was crucified. Jesus told them plainly He was going to lay down His life as a ransom for sinners (Matt. 16:21), but they were still bewildered when Jesus' dead body was laid in a tomb, lifeless, bruised, pale, and cold. How could men who spent three years with Jesus be baffled about who He was and what He came to do?

With hindsight, it is easy to judge people for being confused about Jesus. Knowing the whole story allows us to wonder, "How could they not know that Jesus was the fulfillment of hundreds of Old Testament prophecies?"

Perhaps they would have known that Jesus was indeed the Messiah who came to be the Savior of the world if they had just known their Old Testament better.

The Road to Emmaus

Jesus died on the Cross on Friday at 3 p.m. The city of Jerusalem fell silent for the Saturday Sabbath. The town was especially quiet as it was the Passover Sabbath. When Sunday morning (the first day of the Jewish week) arrived, the city was not the only thing that came to life.

Jesus Christ raised Himself from the dead. His tomb was empty. His body was missing and confusion was rampant. Luke picks up the story.

And behold, two of them were going that very day to a village named Emmaus, which was about **seven miles** from Jerusalem. And they were talking with each other about all these things which had taken place. While they were talking and discussing, **Jesus Himself** approached and began traveling with them. But their eyes were prevented from recognizing Him.

And He said to them, "What are these words that you are exchanging with one another as you are walking?"

And they stood still, looking sad. One of them, named Cleopas, answered and said to Him, "**Are You the only one** visiting Jerusalem and unaware of the things which have happened here in these days?"

And He said to them, "What things?"

And they said to Him, "The things about Jesus the Nazarene, who was a **prophet** mighty in deed and word in the sight of God and all the people, and how the chief priests and our rulers delivered Him to the sentence of death, and **crucified Him**. But we were hoping that it was He who was going to redeem Israel. Indeed, besides all this, it is the third day since these things happened. But also some women among us amazed us. When they were at the tomb early in the morning, and **did not find His body**, they came, saying that they had also seen a vision of angels who said that He was alive. Some of those who were with us went to the tomb and found it just exactly as the women also had said; but Him they did not see."

And He said to them, "O foolish men and slow of heart to believe in all that the prophets have spoken! Was it not necessary for the **Christ to suffer** these things and to enter into His glory?"

Then beginning with Moses and with all the prophets, He explained to them **the things concerning Himself in all the Scriptures** (Luke 24:13–27).

What does this mean? It means that Jesus Christ, who lived from approximately A.D. 0 to 33 was spoken about in each and every book of the Old Testament written centuries before He was born. In other words, Jesus used the Old Testament Scriptures to prove that He was indeed the promised Savior of the world.

The Bible Is Axiomatic

You can know that the Bible is true because it is axiomatic, self proving.

If I said, "I think the authors of the Declaration of Independence were brilliant," would it be fair to study the Declaration to see if it is a brilliant document? Similarly, if I said, "I think the Bible is so brilliant, it must be supernatural," would it be fair to look inside of it to see if it is brilliant and supernatural?

To prove that the president lives in the White House only requires us to look inside the windows of 1600 Pennsylvania Avenue. Likewise, it is entirely legitimate to prove that God "lives" in the Bible by looking into the book itself. When we peer into the contents of Scripture, we see such brilliance, it proves definitively that God wrote a book and Jesus is the leading character.

While you and I cannot recreate the steps taken from Jerusalem to Emmaus, we can have the same experience of the two men who walked seven miles with Jesus. We can examine the Old Testament Scriptures to see if Jesus Christ is indeed the truth.

If it is true that one book was written over fifteen hundred years by 40 authors about one man, that would be impressive. If that book made hundreds of predictions about that man which were fulfilled to the letter, that would be supernatural. That is exactly what the Bible is: a book about one man, supernaturally fulfilling hundreds of prophecies. That man is Jesus Christ.

Arguing over Carpet Color

If you have ever watched congressional sessions on CSPAN, you know that men rarely agree on anything. Couples get divorced because they cannot live in peace. Churches split over which carpet to use in the lobby.

Because the Bible was written over the course of fifteen hundred years by 40 different men, we should see complete chaos and disagreement. Instead, we see a theme that is consistent and unmistakable. That theme is Jesus.

Jesus walked seven miles from Jerusalem to Emmaus explaining to two men that the Old Testament was written about Him. Jesus opened up the Scriptures to prove that He was the One they were writing about.

Prepare to take the same walk. Prepare to see Jesus revealed in the Old Testament. Prepare to take a whirlwind tour through the Bible and see the perfect, brilliant harmony that proves, beyond the shadow of a doubt, that Jesus is indeed, the Truth.

250	○
	A.D. 33: Jesus crucified
	A.D. 30: Jesus begins ministry
	A.D. 26: John the Baptist begins preaching
0	○ 0: Jesus is born
	397–5 B.C.: The silent years
250	○
	397 B.C.: Malachi is Israel's last prophet until John the Baptist
500	○ 515 B.C.: Jerusalem rebuilt and temple completed
	536 B.C.: Jews start returning to Jerusalem
	586 B.C.: Southern Kingdom falls to Babylon
750	○ 721 B.C.: Northern Kingdom falls to Assyria
	975 B.C.: Israel split in two
1000	○ 1004 B.C.: Solomon's temple completed
	1015 B.C.: Solomon becomes king
	1055 B.C.: David becomes king
1250	○
	1451 B.C.: The Jews enter the Promised Land
	1491–1451 B.C.: The Jews wander the desert
1500	○ 1491 B.C.: Moses leads the Exodus out of Egypt
	1700–1574 B.C.: Joseph and his brothers have lots of babies
1750	○ 1739 B.C.: Joseph sold into slavery in Egypt
	1836 B.C.: Jacob born
	1896 B.C.: Isaac born
2000	○ 1996 B.C. Abraham born
2250	○
	2349 B.C.: Noah and the Global Flood
2500	○
2750	○
3000	○
3250	○
3500	○
3750	○
4000	○
	4004 B.C.: Creation, Adam and Eve, Cain and Abel

Timeline
4004 B.C. — A.D. 33

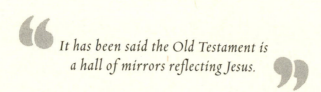

It has been said the Old Testament is a hall of mirrors reflecting Jesus.

Chapter Three

Big, Fancy Words

If you, like I, have ADH whatever it is, you will love this. You are going to read almost one thousand chapters of the Bible in just a few paragraphs. That's right, you are going to zoom through four thousand years of history in a matter of minutes.

Fancy Word Alert

But (you knew that was coming) before you blitzkrieg through the Bible, you are going to get bombed with some fancy theological terms. Some people might say this is unprofitable, but understanding big theological words can be beneficial in three ways:

> You will score big points in Scrabble if you ever get to use one of these whoppers.

> You will see that Christianity is not an ignorant religion for feebleminded people.

> The Bible will explode as you read it. It will come to life for you in ways you never imagined.

Supralapsarianism

Here is your first fancy word that will impress your friends and neighbors: Supralapsarianism. Say what?

Supralapsarianism (and its cousin, infralapsarianism) logically defines the order of God's thinking regarding the creation of the world. What does that have to do with the price of tea in Texas on a Tuesday? It tells you what the purpose of your existence is.

There are three great philosophical questions that every philosopher since Sophocles has pondered:

1. Where did I come from?
2. Why am I here?
3. Where am I going when I die?

Supralapsarianism answers all three questions.

1. God thought of you before the foundation of the world.
2. You are here to glorify God by believing in Him and His Son, Jesus Christ, and live in a way that is pleasing to the One who made you and owns you.
3. If you repent and trust Jesus, your sins will be forgiven and you will go to heaven to enjoy your maker forever. If you do not repent, your sins will not be forgiven, and God, the just judge of all the earth, will sentence you, the guilty criminal, to hell.

Supralapsarianism tells us that God created the world knowing humans would sin in order to send His Son to redeem a people for Himself. Saving sinners was not God's afterthought because Adam and Eve took a nosh of fruit. Saving sinners through the Lord Jesus Christ was God's eternal plan before He even created the earth.

The Bible is God's history book telling us how that plan of redemption unfolded. Everything we read in the Bible is ultimately about God's plan to forgive rebels through Jesus Christ.

Second Fancy Word: Progressive Revelation

The following sentence may win the award for the most obvious statement ever made: History doesn't happen in an instant, it takes time. You are probably thinking, "Duh!"

Sometimes we have a tendency to forget about time as we read the Bible. The story of redemption doesn't happen instantaneously; it took time. Furthermore, God did not reveal His exact plan of salvation in every detail at creation. Instead, He progressively revealed His plan little by little.

The Bible starts out with very fuzzy pictures about the plan of salvation that becomes progressively clearer. Jesus' Apostle, Peter, explained it this way:

> As to this salvation, the prophets who prophesied of the grace that would come to you made careful searches and inquiries, **seeking to know what person or time** the Spirit of Christ within them was indicating as He **predicted the sufferings of Christ** and the glories to follow. It was revealed to them that they were not serving themselves, but you, in these things which now have been announced to you through those who preached the gospel to you by the Holy Spirit sent from heaven — things into which angels **long to look** (1 Pet. 1:10–12).

In the Old Testament, God slowly revealed more and more information about Himself and His plans to save sinners. Even angels didn't know exactly how the story of redemption was going to unfold.

> But when the **fullness of the time came**, God sent forth His Son, born of a woman, born under the Law, so that He might redeem those who were under the Law, that we might receive the adoption as sons (Gal. 4:4–5).

Give or take, God created the world approximately 4000 B.C. He spent the next four millennia rolling out His plan of redemption. The Old Testament is a history of a chosen nation called Israel, which would produce a Messiah who would suffer and die for sinners (Isa. 53).

Israel was to be a set-apart nation, different from all of her neighbors because God wanted a holy nation to be the country that delivered the Son of God to save the world. As you read the Old Testament, that is what you are reading: God's story of redemption through a chosen people.

It was at the exact right time that God finally sent His Son to be born in Israel to redeem the world. When Jesus Christ began His ministry of redemption, He announced, "**The time is fulfilled**, and the Kingdom of God is at hand; repent and believe in the Gospel" (Mark 1:15).

The Old Testament progressively led to a culmination in Jesus and here is the kicker: the New Testament points to a climax in the future that involves you.

Third Fancy Word: Typology

How exactly did God progressively reveal His plan of salvation in Jesus Christ throughout the Old Testament? He did it through prophecies (predictions of future events) and through our third fancy theological term: *typology*, also known as types and shadows.

It has been said the Old Testament is a hall of mirrors reflecting Jesus. Theologians take their cue from Jesus Himself when He spoke to the Pharisees in John chapter 5:

> You search the Scriptures because you think that in them you have eternal life; it is these that **testify about Me** (John 5:39).

While there is some wisdom literature (Job, Psalms, Proverbs, etc.), the Old Testament is actually a history book with theology in it. There are no true allegories (fictional events that teach a lesson), but there are actual events that are fuzzy pictures of something else. This is called "types" and "shadows."

Is the shadow of an object the real thing? No, it is merely a shadowy representation of the real thing, but it is not the object itself. If I stand in your shadow, am I standing in you? No, I am merely standing in a less-than-perfect representation of you. In the Old Testament, God shares stories with us that are shadowy pictures (or types) of the real thing. The real thing is Jesus.

Types can be a person, object, office, ceremony, structure, or event which is a fuzzy picture of Jesus. The "type" is an Old Testament shadow of the clearer "anti-type" Jesus in the New Testament. Even though the type is an actual person, place, or thing, the anti-type is always greater and more clear than the type. The picture is never as clear as the actual subject.

Here is the New Testament verse that makes this fuzzy concept very clear:

> Therefore no one is to act as your judge in regard to food or drink or in respect to a festival or a new moon or a Sabbath day — things which are a mere **shadow** of **what is to come**; but **the substance** belongs to **Christ** (Col. 2:16–17).

Old Testament festivals and the Sabbath were shadowy pictures of Jesus Christ. Other verses in the New Testament identify even more shadowy Old Testament pictures of Jesus: people, places, things, events, offices. While some people go looking for Jesus in every verse in the Old Testament, we are going to limit our examination to just the types and shadows that are identified as such in the New Testament.

Why?

Why did God do it this way? Why did God wait four thousand years to send Jesus to redeem the world? Why didn't He just create the world, let us sin, and then send Jesus right away?

Imagine a man who stood in Times Square today and shouted, "I am God. Repent and believe in ME." We would think him a madman.

Two thousand years ago, that is exactly what Jesus did. He stood in the marketplace and called Himself God. Why should we listen to Him? Why should we not consider Him a crackpot?

Jesus was not a crazy street preacher without a basis in history. Jesus' history doesn't start in Matthew 1, it starts in Genesis 1.

1. Jesus has the history of a set-apart nation.
2. Jesus has the history of a religion.
3. Jesus has the history of a God who performed miracles.
4. Jesus has the foundation of a book.
5. Jesus is the fulfillment of dozens of prophecies predicting where He would be born and how He would live and die.

Because Jesus was the fulfillment of four thousand years of expectations, Jesus was not a Time's Square crackpot.

Bad Grammar

Let's put all of our fancy words together in one run-on sentence: God's pre-eternal plan of salvation is revealed to us in a progressive revelation that established Jesus' words and miracles as more than a show but as a fulfillment with a history and a foundation through a series of types and shadows in the Old Testament revealed in the New Testament anti-type, the Lord Jesus Christ.

You are about to see those types and shadows. You are about to see fuzzy Old Testament pictures made clear in the person of Jesus Christ. Prepare to witness the amazing consistency and prophetic nature of the Bible. Prepare to see the unmasked Jesus.

Human history begins with two shadows of God's prearranged plan to rescue us.

Chapter Four

The Scarlet Thread in the Old Testament

Let's begin in the beginning.

Two Naked Vegetarians

We don't know the exact date of creation, but let's call it 4000 B.C. God spoke the entire universe into existence and He called it very good (Gen. 1:31). Because everything was "very good" and there was no sin, the first humans were two unashamed naked vegetarians named Adam and Eve. They lived in a beautiful garden, communing with God. There was a river and two trees. God gave them a single rule: Don't eat from that one tree or you will die (Gen. 2:17).

Yes, Adam and Eve were perfect, but if God had not given them free wills, then obeying God would have been a coerced, forced obedience. God gave them one rule to obey: don't eat that!

Unfortunately, that rascally devil came along and tempted them to eat the fruit from the forbidden tree.

> When the woman saw that the tree was good for food, and that it was a delight to the eyes, and that the tree was desirable to make one wise, she took from its fruit and **ate**; and she gave also to her husband with her, and he **ate**. Then the eyes of both of them were opened, and they knew that **they were naked**; and they sewed fig leaves together and made themselves loin **coverings** (Gen. 3:6–7).

This was no ordinary boo-boo. Our two naked vegetarians had everything in the world, but they still rebelled against God. What was their first response to their major league hiccup? To cover up their nakedness and shame with fig leaves. They chose fig leaves because they were vegetarians; they would never think to kill an animal to make a leather covering.

When God informed them of the consequences for their sin, we see the first shadowy reference that He will rescue mankind from the death they deserve for disobeying Him.

God spoke to the devil and said, "And I will put enmity between you and the woman, and between your seed and her seed; He shall **bruise you** on the head, and **you shall bruise him** on the heel" (Gen. 3:15).

Who Is He?

This was a shadowy reference that Eve would have a human descendant (He) who would crush the work of the devil, but it will cause that human a great deal of pain (a bruised heel). Theologians call this verse the proto-evangelium, the first Gospel. While certainly not a complete picture of salvation, it is the first time the Gospel is promised. That promise was given immediately after mans' fall into sin.

The Gospel begins in Genesis. The Cross is foreshadowed at creation. The Old Testament is not a bunch of haphazard stories strung together until a man named Jesus showed up. Because the story of the Bible is the story about Christ, He makes a fuzzy appearance immediately at creation.

Immediately after promising a Savior, God cast another shadow. "The LORD God made **garments of skin** for Adam and his wife, and **clothed them**" (Gen. 3:21).

The first animals ever butchered were killed by God Himself. Man's effort to cover his own shame with fig leaves was not acceptable to God, so He shed the first blood that was ever spilt for the covering of man's sin.

There are five crucial lessons to be learned from this:

1. Sin is very serious. Sin is violation of God's law (1 John 3:4). Because God is so holy, so perfect, so righteous, so just, even the slightest infraction of His law is worthy of eternal punishment. Why? Because our sins are committed against the One who is eternally perfect.

2. Because God is loving, He has righteous anger toward sin (Ps. 7:11). He has a settled, determined wrath that will be poured out to satisfy the demands of the law. God is not capricious. He does not fly off the handle when we sin. He is a calm, just God who is the perfect accountant. Not a single sin will fall through the cracks. There will be a day of justice when every single violation of His law will be accounted for (2 Cor. 5:10).

3. Man's efforts to appease the wrath of God are not sufficient. Not only are our efforts not enough to satisfy His demand for justice, our good works are actually seen as contaminated offerings. All of our righteous deeds are like a "filthy garment" (Isa. 64:6) because they are offered from sinful, contaminated hands. We can do nothing to satisfy the righteous demands of a righteous God. Left to ourselves we are without hope.

4. We need God to intervene and rescue us.

5. We need a perfect blood sacrifice. We need a perfect man to represent sinful man, and we need the sacrifice of God Himself to appease the wrath of God Himself. We need a God-man to shed His blood for the forgiveness of our sins.

Human history begins with two shadows of God's prearranged plan to rescue us. These are shadowy pictures indeed, but the shadows slowly lift.

Still Approximately 4,000 Years Before Christ

The very next Bible story picks up our shadowy theme. Genesis 4 is the true story of Adam and Eve's first two sons.

Cain and Abel both offered a sacrifice to God. Cain offered God a grain offering while his brother Abel brought choice selections from his flock.

> And the LORD **had regard** for Abel and for his offering; but for Cain and for his offering He had **no regard** (Gen. 4:4–5).

God was pleased with the sacrifice of an animal offered in faith, but He was not pleased with a grain offering. We see that God's "sacrifice of choice" is a blood-bearing animal. The shadow becomes just slightly less fuzzy.

2,050 Years Before Christ

God's shadowy prearranged plan unfolds with a man named Abraham. God called Abraham to be the father of a great nation (Israel) by providing aged Abraham with a son. One day, God tested the faith of Abraham. On the surface this event may sound strange to us, but this event happened as a shadow of things to come.

God commanded Abraham to do something that He had forbidden: sacrifice a human being. God told Abraham to sacrifice his precious son, Isaac.

Abraham traveled to **Mount Moriah** (the mountain right outside of the not-yet-built city of Jerusalem) with Isaac and two of his servants.

> Abraham said to his young men, "Stay here with the donkey, and I and the lad will go over there; and we will worship and return to you." Abraham took the wood of the burnt offering and **laid it on Isaac** his son, and he took in his hand the fire and the knife. So the two of them walked on together. Isaac spoke to Abraham his father and said, "My **father!**" And he said, "Here I am, **my son.**" And he said, "Behold, the fire and the wood, but **where is the lamb** for the burnt offering?" Abraham said, "**God will provide for Himself the lamb** for the burnt offering, my son." So the two of them walked on together (Gen. 22:5–8).

Abraham prepared to sacrifice his son and God intervened.

> He said, "Do not stretch out your hand against the lad, and do nothing to him; for now I know that you fear God, since you have not withheld your son, **your only son**, from Me." Then Abraham raised his eyes and looked, and behold, behind him a **ram** caught in the thicket by his horns; and Abraham went and took the ram and offered him up for a burnt offering **in the place of his son.** Abraham called the name of that place **The LORD Will Provide**, as it is said to this day, "In the mount of the LORD **it will be provided**" (Gen. 22:12–14).

Two thousand years before God's Son, Jesus Christ, came to this earth, God gave us a shadowy picture of the death of another beloved son in Jerusalem. In this shadowy picture, the son was spared. The next time the sacrifice of a son was required, blood would be shed. That blood would be from the lamb that God would provide.

1,446 Years Before Christ

The Jews are now captive in Egypt working as slaves. God rescued them by sending ten plagues to Pharaoh. The first nine plagues failed to soften Pharaoh's heart, so God sent plague number ten and it was a doozey. God threatened Pharaoh, "If you don't let my people go, I will kill every firstborn child" (Exodus 11:4–8). However, God provided a way for the Israelites to escape the death of their firstborn children.

> Speak to all the congregation of Israel, saying, "On the tenth of this month they are each one to take a **lamb** for themselves, according to their fathers' households. . . . Your lamb shall be an **unblemished male** a year old; you may take it from the sheep or from the goats. You shall keep it until the fourteenth day of the same month, then the whole assembly of the congregation of Israel is to **kill it** at twilight. Moreover, they shall take some of the **blood** and put it on the two doorposts and on the lintel of the houses in which they eat it. . . . For I will go through the land of Egypt on that night, and will strike down all the firstborn in the land of Egypt, both man and beast. . . . The **blood** shall be a sign for you on the houses where you live; and when I see the **blood** I will **pass over** you (Exod. 12:3–13).

A spotless lamb would dwell with a family for a short time and then the family would kill the lamb without breaking any of the lamb's bones. The blood of a lamb would cause the angel of death to pass over those who put their trust in God. Shadowy, but clearer.

Jesus Christ came and dwelt with His people for a short time. He was spotless and His own killed Him. Despite the fact that He was brutally beaten and had nails pounded through His hands and feet, not a bone in His body was broken. It is the blood of Jesus that provides forgiveness of sins and allows us to escape spiritual death.

1,444 Years Before Christ

The Jews had been delivered from Egypt and they were at the foot of Mount Sinai. God provided a long list of rules for the people to obey. God instructed the priests to make an annual sacrifice for the covering of people's sins: this was called the Day of Atonement (Yom Kippur).

On this day, the priests would lay their hands on the head of an unblemished lamb, signifying the transfer of sins from the human to the lamb. Then they would slit the throat of the lamb and it would bleed to death for the *covering* of their sins.

More Blood

By now you might be wondering what's up with all the blood?

> For the life of the flesh is in the **blood**, and I have given it to you on the altar to make **atonement** for your souls; for it is the **blood** by reason of the life that makes **atonement** (Lev. 17:11).

Just imagine the amount of blood that was shed over the centuries. This was a constant reminder to the Jewish people that blood was required for the covering of sins. Unfortunately for them, a lamb could not forgive sins.

Because a lamb doesn't know if he is on his way to get a haircut or to become a lamb chop, a lamb sacrifice only served as a covering for sin. That is what Yom Kippur means — a Day of Covering. Even though millions of lambs were sacrificed, this was merely a picture of a need for a greater sacrifice for the complete forgiveness of sins.

The shadowy picture of sacrificial lambs is becoming progressively clearer.

600 Years before Christ

For the next eight hundred years, the children of Israel lived under this sacrificial covenant system. Because this system covered but didn't remove their sins, people still lived with guilt. Despite rivers of blood from lamb sacrifices, forgiveness was still longed for.

Suddenly, a prophet named Jeremiah announced a new covenant that would FORGIVE their sins and remove their guilt once and for all. Needless to say, this was a big announcement.

> I will **forgive** their iniquity, and their sin I will remember **no more** (Jer. 31:34).

God announced a brand-new way to have sins not just covered, but forgiven. The question was, how would God do this? The prophet Isaiah gives us more than a hint by describing a coming Messiah. Keep in mind, this was written over six hundred years before Jesus Christ was born.

> He has no stately form or majesty that we should look upon Him, nor appearance that we should be attracted to Him. He was **despised** and forsaken of men, a man of sorrows and acquainted

with grief; and like one from whom men hide their face He was **despised**, and **we did not esteem Him**. Surely **our** griefs He Himself bore, and **our** sorrows He carried; yet we ourselves esteemed Him stricken, smitten of God, and afflicted. But He was pierced through **for our transgressions**, He was crushed **for our iniquities**; the chastening for our well-being fell upon Him, and **by His scourging we are healed**. All of us like sheep have gone astray, each of us has turned to his own way; but **the Lord has caused** the iniquity of us all to fall on Him.

He was oppressed and He was afflicted, yet He **did not open His mouth**; like a **lamb** that is led to slaughter, and like a **sheep** that is silent before its shearers, so He **did not open His mouth**. By oppression and **judgment** He was taken away; and as for His generation, who considered that **He was cut off out of the land of the living** for the transgression of my people, to whom the stroke was due? (Isa. 53:2–8).

Isaiah concluded this amazing description of a murdered Messiah with this shocking statement, "But the Lord was **pleased to crush Him**, putting Him to grief" (Isa. 53:10). There it is again. Seven centuries before Jesus came to this earth, Isaiah announced the Lord's prearranged plan of salvation; to sacrifice a spotless lamb for the forgiveness of sins.

The shadow is getting very clear.

430 Years before Christ

It is now two hundred years after Jeremiah announced a new covenant for the forgiveness of sins by a lamb-like Messiah. No Messiah has arrived yet. Where is He? Who is He? The very last book of the Old Testament ends like this, "Behold, I am going to send you Elijah the prophet before the coming of the great and terrible day of the LORD" (Mal. 4:5).

That is how the Old Testament closes, and then . . . nothing.

For four hundred years God did not send this promised prophet to reveal the Messiah. The Jews were left in the shadows and with their guilt. So they faithfully sacrificed lamb after lamb after lamb after lamb for the covering of their sins.

250

A.D. 33: Jesus crucified
A.D. 30: Jesus begins ministry
A.D. 26: John the Baptist begins preaching

0

0: Jesus is born

397–5 B.C.: The silent years

250

397 B.C.: Malachi is Israel's last prophet until John the Baptist

500

515 B.C.: Jerusalem rebuilt and temple completed
536 B.C.: Jews start returning to Jerusalem
586 B.C.: Southern Kingdom falls to Babylon
721 B.C.: Northern Kingdom falls to Assyria

750

975 B.C.: Israel split in two

1000

1004 B.C.: Solomon's temple completed
1015 B.C.: Solomon becomes king
1055 B.C.: David becomes king

1250

1451 B.C.: The Jews enter the Promised Land
1491–1451 B.C.: The Jews wander the desert
1491 B.C.: Moses leads the Exodus out of Egypt

1500

1700–1574 B.C.: Joseph and his brothers have lots of babies
1739 B.C.: Joseph sold into slavery in Egypt

1750

1836 B.C.: Jacob born
1896 B.C.: Isaac born
1996 B.C.: Abraham born

2000

2250

2349 B.C.: Noah and the Global Flood

2500

2750

3000

3250

Timeline
4004 B.C. — A.D. 33

3500

3750

4000

4004 B.C.: Creation, Adam and Eve, Cain and Abel

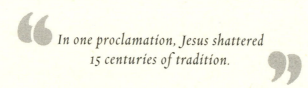

*In one proclamation, Jesus shattered
15 centuries of tradition.*

Chapter Five

The Scarlet Thread in the New Testament

Few of us have the patience for waiting. Imagine waiting four hundred years for someone. Okay, you would be dead, but that's not the point.

God promised the Jews a Messiah who would save people from their sins (Matt. 1:21), but that was hundreds of years ago. Where is this Promised One? What is taking so long?

God's bloody sacrificial system in the Old Testament provided for the covering of sins. But the sacrificing of lambs never removed guilt; it was only a shadowy picture of a better sacrifice to come; a sacrifice that would forgive sins.

Year after year, lamb after lamb, the Jews shed blood for the covering of sins.

30 Anno Domini (the Year of Our Lord)

After four hundred years of complete silence and countless blood sacrifices, God spoke. He sent an Elijah-type prophet named John the Baptist who pointed at Jesus Christ and announced,

> "Behold! The **Lamb** of God who **takes away** the sin of the world!" (John 1:29).

After centuries of longing for a Messiah to deliver them from their sins, Jesus Christ, the Lamb of God, appeared. Suddenly, the shadows of the Old Testament are revealed as pictures of Jesus Christ who came to this earth to be the perfect sacrifice for the complete forgiveness of sins.

Just as the scarlet thread ran through the Old Testament, that same theme makes its way through the entire New Testament. Old Testament lambs were sacrificed repeatedly for the covering of sins. The better New Testament Lamb would be sacrificed one time for the forgiveness of sins.

33 Anno Domini (the Year of Our Lord)

For fifteen hundred years the Jews had been celebrating Passover by killing an unblemished male lamb and partaking in a Passover meal. Many foods would be eaten symbolically, like bitter herbs to remind them of their bitter sufferings under the Egyptians. They would also drink wine at four different times throughout the meal. The third cup of wine was a toast to the lamb whose blood had been shed that day for the covering of their sins.

It was Passover week in the year A.D. 33 and Jesus was in the city of Jerusalem to celebrate the night the death angel passed over the children of Israel if they had sacrificed a lamb and put the lamb's blood on their doorpost. On the night Jesus was going to be arrested, He reclined at a table in Jerusalem to eat the Passover meal with His 12 disciples.

> For I received from the Lord that which I also delivered to you, that the Lord Jesus in the night in which He was betrayed took bread; and when He had given thanks, He broke it and said, "This is **My body**, which is for you; do this in remembrance of Me." In the same way He took the cup also after supper, saying, "This cup is the **new covenant in My blood**; do this, as often as you drink it, in remembrance of Me." For as often as you eat this bread and drink the cup, you proclaim the Lord's death until He comes (1 Cor. 11:23–26).

By uttering these words, Jesus basically proclaimed, "Don't toast the lambs that could merely cover sins. Toast Me, the Lamb of God who takes away the sins of the world."

In one proclamation, Jesus shattered 15 centuries of tradition. No longer would a continual stream of animal blood be shed for the covering of sins; Jesus Christ would be sacrificed one time for the complete forgiveness of sins.

This must have stunned the disciples. With one sentence, Jesus announced the fulfillment of the old covenant and the creation of a new covenant promised over six hundred years ago by the prophet Jeremiah.

Not only must His announcement have flabbergasted the disciples, but it must have shocked and grieved them. Jesus made the fuzzy picture clear, the Old Testament lambs were mere types and shadows of Him. Jesus was going to willingly and knowingly sacrifice Himself to save sinners.

Two thousand years ago, Jesus Christ, the Lamb of God, was murdered in fulfillment of God's pre-arranged plan. While there is no intrinsic power in the actual blood of Jesus, His shed blood is enough to cleanse anyone who comes to Him in repentance and faith. The blood that was shed two thousand years ago has the same power today.

Today

Not only does the Bible tell us about the past, the Scriptures tell us what Jesus is doing right now. Surprise — the scarlet thread continues!

So Christ has now become the **High Priest** over all the good things that have come. He has entered that great, perfect sanctuary in heaven, not made by human hands and not part of this created world. **Once for all time He took blood** into that Most Holy Place, but not the blood of goats and calves. He took His own blood, and with it He secured our salvation forever.

Under the old system, the blood of goats and bulls and the ashes of a young cow could cleanse people's bodies from ritual defilement.

Just think how much more the **blood of Christ will purify our hearts** from deeds that lead to death so that we can worship the living God. For by the power of the eternal Spirit, Christ offered himself to God as a **perfect sacrifice for our sins**.

That is why He is the one who *mediates the **new covenant*** between God and people, so that all who are invited can receive the eternal inheritance that God has promised them. For Christ died to **set them free** from the penalty of the sins they had committed under that first covenant (Heb. 9:11–15).

Right now, Jesus Christ is ensuring that people who repent and trust Him will have His good work credited to their accounts so they can be forgiven for their crimes against God and be spared from the wrath that is to come (Heb. 12:24).

The blood that Jesus shed two thousand years ago is still efficacious. Jesus' blood still has the power to forgive sinners and keep them forgiven.

The Bible doesn't stop there! The Bible progressively reveals what is going to happen in the future.

Someday Soon

The last book of the Bible is an apocalyptic vision of the Apostle John that tells us how God is going to unfold His prearranged plan for His glory. Let's pull back the curtain on the future and see what role you will play in glorifying God.

> Then I looked, and I heard the voice of many angels around the throne and the living creatures and the elders; and the number of them was myriads of myriads, and thousands of thousands, saying with a loud voice, "Worthy is the **Lamb** that was **slain** to receive power and riches and wisdom and might and honor and glory and blessing."
>
> And every created thing which is in heaven and on the earth and under the earth and on the sea, and all things in them, I heard saying, "To Him who sits on the throne, and to the **Lamb**, be blessing and honor and glory and dominion forever and ever."
>
> And the four living creatures kept saying, "Amen." And the elders fell down and worshiped (Rev. 5:11–14).

We don't need "trip to heaven" books. We have an actual God-ordained vision of heaven and future events. In the future, Jesus Christ, the Lamb of God, will receive the praises of all the creatures in heaven, and then the end of time will come.

> I looked when **He** broke the sixth seal, and there was a great earthquake; and the sun became black as sackcloth made of hair, and the whole moon became like blood; and the stars of the sky fell to the earth, as a fig tree casts its unripe figs when shaken by a great wind. The sky was split apart like a scroll when it is rolled up, and every mountain and island were moved out of their places. Then the kings of the earth and the great men and the commanders and the

rich and the strong and every slave and free man hid themselves in the caves and among the rocks of the mountains; and they said to the mountains and to the rocks, "**Fall on us** and hide us from the presence of Him who sits on the throne, and from **the wrath of the Lamb**; for the great day of their wrath has come, and who is able to stand?" (Rev. 6:12–17).

When Jesus returns to this earth, He will judge the world in righteousness. Remember, God's character demands that justice is satisfied and every single evil deed punished. This is what judgment day will look like for unforgiven sinners, and there is nothing shadowy about this.

> Then I saw a **great white throne** and **Him** who sat upon it, from whose presence earth and heaven fled away, and no place was found for them. And I saw the dead, the great and the small, standing before the throne, and **books were opened**; and another book was opened, which is the book of life; and the dead were judged from the things which were written in the books, according to their deeds. And the sea gave up the dead which were in it, and death and Hades gave up the dead which were in them; and **they were judged**, every one of them according to their deeds. Then death and Hades **were thrown** into the lake of fire. This is the second death, the lake of fire. And if anyone's name was not found written in the book of life, he **was thrown** into the lake of fire (Rev. 20:11–15).

Jesus warned that the majority of people will find themselves thrown to hell for their sins (Matt. 7:13–14). When He returns, He will stand as judge of those whose sins are not forgiven. Every sin will be accounted for. Every blasphemous word will be punished. Every filthy deed will receive its due.

Notice that unforgiven sinners will not "fall" to hell, they will be thrown. Can you guess who does the throwing? There will not be a trap door with a chute that leads sinners to hell like a waterpark slide. God Himself will cast them to eternal damnation.

Once sinners arrive at the lake of sulfur, they will suffer eternal, conscious torment glorifying God as He pours out His wrath on sinners.

> Then He will also say to those on His left, "Depart from Me, **accursed ones**, into the **eternal fire** which has **been prepared** for the devil and his angels (Matt. 25:41).

Hell didn't evolve, it was prepared. By God. The flames of hell do not stay lit by themselves, they are fueled by God. Because He is glorified by everything, God will be glorified in the death of sinners. It is a small glory, but He will be glorified.

Great News

For those whose names are securely written in the Lamb's Book of Life, for those whose sins are forgiven, God's prearranged plan is amazing.

> Then I saw a **new** heaven and a **new** earth; for the first heaven and the first earth passed away, and there is no longer any sea. And I saw the holy city, **new** Jerusalem, coming down out of heaven from God, made ready as a bride adorned for her husband. And I heard a loud voice from the throne, saying, "Behold, the tabernacle of God is among men, and **He will dwell among them**, and they shall be His people, and God Himself will be among them, and He will wipe away **every tear** from their eyes; and there will **no longer be any death**; there will no longer be any mourning, or crying, or pain; the first things have passed away."
>
> And He who sits on the throne [Jesus] said, "Behold, I am making all things new." And He said, "Write, for these words are **faithful and true**." Then He said to me, "It is done. I am the Alpha and the Omega, the beginning and the end. I will give to the one who thirsts from the spring of the water of life **without cost**. He who overcomes will inherit these things, and I will be his God and he will be My son. But for the cowardly and unbelieving and abominable and murderers and immoral persons and sorcerers and idolaters and all liars, their part will be in the **lake that burns with fire and brimstone**, which is the second death" (Rev. 21:1–8).

What will heaven be like and who will be there?

> And the twelve gates were twelve pearls; each one of the gates was a single pearl. And the street of the city was pure gold, like transparent glass.
>
> I saw no temple in it, for the Lord God the Almighty and the **Lamb are its temple**. And the city has no need of the sun or of the moon to shine on it, for the glory of God has illumined it, and its **lamp is the Lamb**. The nations will walk by its light, and the kings of the earth will bring their glory into it. In the daytime (for there

will be no night there) its gates will never be closed; and they will bring the glory and the honor of the nations into it; and nothing unclean, and no one who practices abomination and lying, shall ever come into it, but only those whose names are written in the **Lamb's book of life** (Rev. 21:21–27).

The last chapter in the Bible hearkens back to the very beginning of the Bible. The Garden of Eden was perfect and it contained a river and two trees. God's people communed perfectly in the actual presence of God.

Here is the last chapter of the Bible as it describes the new heavens in the future.

Then he showed me a **river** of the water of life, clear as crystal, coming from the throne of God and of **the Lamb**, in the middle of its street. On either side of the river was the **tree of life**, bearing twelve kinds of fruit, yielding its fruit every month; and the leaves of the tree were for the healing of the nations. There will no longer be any curse; and the throne of God and of the **Lamb** will be in it, and His bond-servants will serve Him; they will see His face, and His name will be on their foreheads. And there will no longer be any night; and they will not have need of the light of a lamp nor the light of the sun, because the Lord God will illumine them; and **they will reign** forever and ever.

And he said to me, "These words are **faithful** and **true**"; and the Lord, the God of the spirits of the prophets, sent His angel to show to His bond-servants the things which must soon take place (Rev. 22:1–6).

Is the Angel Right?

Are these words "trustworthy and true?"

You have just read the biblical history of redemption and God's future plan for the world. Is it true?

You cannot be postmodern about this. You cannot say that this is "true for you but it is not true for me." That is not an option. Why? Jesus didn't make it an option when He said that He is "the way, and the truth, and the life; no one comes to the Father but through Me" (John 14:6).

The postmodern worldview collapses under Jesus' exclusive truth claim. It makes no sense to say that His statement is true for some but not for others. If it is someone's truth that EVERYONE will be judged and either be found guilty or in Christ, that means you are a part of the EVERYONE.

Nobody is exempt from this scenario. You simply cannot dismiss Jesus' claim by stating, "That may be true for you, but not for me." If it is true for me, then you will be included.

There is no escaping this: the biblical story of Jesus is either false or true.

Where Is Your Name Written?

Everything that God has done and is doing in this world is to bring honor to Himself. Humans exist to glorify Him by either receiving His mercy, grace, and lovingkindness, or by receiving His wrath.

The Bible is a supernatural book that foretold the death and Resurrection of Jesus Christ as God's plan of redemption. The gazillion-dollar question is, will you be punished in a Lake of Fire or be reigning with the Lamb of God?

Now What?

What must one do to have their name written in the Lamb's Book of Life? You must do what the men of Israel did in Acts chapter 2 when they heard the preaching of the Apostle Peter.

> "Men of Israel, listen to these words: Jesus the Nazarene, a man attested to you by God with miracles and wonders and signs which God performed through Him in your midst, just as you yourselves know— this *Man*, delivered over by the **predetermined plan** and **foreknowledge of God**, you nailed to a cross by the hands of godless men and put Him to death. But God raised Him up again, putting an end to the agony of death, since it was impossible for Him to be held in its power. . . .
>
> "This Jesus God raised up again, to which we are all **witnesses**. . . .
>
> "Therefore let all the house of Israel **know for certain** that God has made Him both Lord and Christ — this Jesus whom you crucified."
>
> Now when they heard this, they were pierced to the heart, and said to Peter and the rest of the apostles, "Brethren, **what shall we do?**" Peter said to them, "**Repent**, and each of you be baptized in the name of Jesus Christ for the forgiveness of your sins; and you will receive the gift of the Holy Spirit. For the **promise** is for you

and your children and **for all** who are far off, as many as the Lord our God will call to Himself" (Acts 2:22–39).

What must you do to be saved? You must repent and put your trust in Jesus. You must turn from your sins and place your faith in Christ as if your life depended on it, because it does.

If you are already a follower of the Lamb, you have much to look forward to.

If you have not repented, what are you waiting for? Why would you delay?

Congratulations!

You just rocketed through four thousand years of human history in two chapters. Well done! Now that we have taken a high-altitude look at the entire Bible, let's touch down throughout the Old Testament to see more types and shadows of Jesus.

As we make our way through the Old Testament, you are going to see three things.

1. Lots of types and shadows of Jesus.
2. The timeline of the Old Testament. You will have a clear understanding of the order of biblical history.
3. Explanations for why the world works the way it does.

Where shall we begin? The beginning is a very nice place to start.

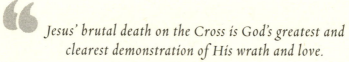

Chapter Six

Jesus Is the Ark

It sure didn't take long for humans to make a hash of things. God created a perfectly perfect earth, Adam and Eve sinned, and the next thing you know, the world is the *Lord of the Flies*.

William Golding's *Lord of the Flies* is a fictional story of a group of boys who survived a plane crash and lived together on a remote island. No adults. No government. No laws.

The result? The civilized British chaps fell into savagery faster than you can say, "Gilligan's Island." One wonders if Golding plagiarized Genesis 6. Less than seventeen hundred years after creation, we read of the depravity of . . . us.

> Then the LORD saw that the **wickedness** of man was great on the earth, and that every intent of the thoughts of his heart was only **evil continually**. The LORD was sorry that He had made man on the earth, and He was grieved in His heart (Gen. 6:5–6).

Contrary to the modern-day self-esteem movement, the people described in Genesis 6 were not a special class of humans; they were people just like you and me. Left to ourselves, we too are evil continually. Nothing has changed.

Totally Depraved

Human beings are not only not perfect, we're bad, we're bad, we're really, really bad. Without the curb of laws, government, and shame, we are not law-abiding citizens, we are wretches like the one the song refers to. "**Every intent** of the thoughts of his heart was only evil continually" (Gen. 6:5).

Just 17 centuries after God created His image bearers, humans were behaving so badly that God was "sorry that He made man on the earth" (Gen. 6:6). That doesn't mean that He made a mistake in creating us, it is simply an anthropomorphic term used for us to understand how God felt about our sin; it grieved Him. This is the first verse in the Bible that tells us God has feelings.

God Has Feelings

God is not ruled by emotions, because He is impassible (without passions), but He does indeed have feelings.

1. God grieves.

> Do not **grieve the Holy Spirit** of God, by whom you were sealed for the day of redemption (Eph. 4:30).

2. God rejoices.

> The LORD your God is in your midst,
> A victorious warrior.
> He will exult over you **with joy**,
> He will be quiet in His love,
> He will **rejoice over you** with shouts of **joy** (Zeph. 3:17).

3. God is angry.

> But because of your stubbornness and unrepentant heart you are storing up **wrath** for yourself in the day of **wrath** and revelation of the righteous judgment of God, who will render to each person according to his deeds: to those who by persever-ance in doing good seek for glory and honor and immortality, eternal life; but to those who are selfishly ambitious and do not

obey the truth, but obey unrighteousness, **wrath** and **indignation** (Rom. 2:5–8).

4. God can be sad.

Jesus wept (John 11:35).

God Is Not Emotional

Even though He has emotions, God is not careening from one emotion to another. He does not whiplash from one sentiment to another. In other words, God is not a teenager.

We get our emotions from God, we certainly didn't evolve them. Why would we? Our emotions come from God because our Maker has emotions.

God has some attributes that are uniquely His (incommunicable attributes):

> He alone is totally powerful: omnipotent (Matt. 19:26).
> He alone is all knowing: omniscient (Isa. 46:10).
> He alone is everywhere: omnipresent (Ps. 139:8).

God also has attributes that we share with Him as image bearers of God (communicable attributes):

> God thinks: we think (Isa. 55:8).
> God works: we work (Ps. 139:13–14).
> God has emotions: we have emotions (cf. above).

God is not emotional, but He has emotions. When He sees the wickedness of man on full display, it displeases Him and grieves Him and even angers Him. Why?

Sin Is Really, Really Sinful

Sin is not simply a violation of His rules, sin is contrary to who He is. God is not merely a judge who sits on a courtroom bench and hands down sentences in compliance to standards written by others. God is the standard.

He did not write the laws as a moral code that He Himself must keep. The laws of God are a perfect representation of His character and nature (Rom. 2:20). God is the law.

When we break a law (lie, steal, murder, fornicate, blaspheme, lust, hate, covet, gossip, dishonor authority) we are striking out at God's character and in essence saying, "I hate who you are." That is why sin is exceedingly sinful (Rom. 7:13).

We Are Naturally Good at It

We are not sinners because we sin; we sin because we are sinners. If man has one innate skill, it is our ability to sin. We sin naturally because our natures are sinful. Pour a carton of milk and milk comes out, because milk is in it.

From birth we are totally depraved (Rom. 5:18–19; Ps. 51:5). Ask your mother.

Just like the humans in Genesis 6, our thoughts are evil continually. Does that mean we sit around plotting how to rule the world? Well, in a sense, yes.

We are not like Hitler, who wanted to rule the planet, but we do want to run our own little fiefdoms. We don't like to be told what to do from birth. To verify that statement, simply visit your local Chuck E Cheese's.

Our desire to run our own universe starts when we take our first gulp of air.

> We cry because we want food. Now.
> We collapse limply to the ground when we are told to go to bed when we don't want to.
> We sulk when our parents tell us we can't have what we want.

We act like little *Lord of the Flies* savages when we are children. Do we need to talk about how we behave when we are teenagers?

Just like the folks in Genesis 6, we sin constantly. No, we don't rob banks or strangle cats, but we sin continually. Wanna bet?

> How many meals have you wolfed down without bowing your head to thank the One who provided it for you?
> How many times have you thanked God for the air that He provides for you?
> How many hours a day do you spend loving God with all of your heart, soul, mind, and strength?
> How many times have you taken God's name in vain?
> How many times did you dishonor your parents?
> How many times have you lusted or looked at pornography?
> How many times have you lied? A recent study claims that the average person lies three times per ten minutes during a conversation.
> How many times have you complained and impugned God's integrity?

> How many times have you desired something that did not belong to you?
> How many times have you driven past a homeless person?
> How many commercials have you seen that show the plight of the hungry and you just keep on clicking?

You get the point. Just like the sinners in Genesis 6, every intent of the thoughts of our hearts are only evil continually. Whether we are aware of it or not, our actions are earning us a reward. Unfortunately, our sinful actions only earn us wrath stored up for us in a little ol' place called hell. Prepare for an understatement: that is a bummer.

Why Sin's Punishment Is Really, Really Bad

While our sins are bad in and of themselves, what makes sin truly horrific is the One against whom we have committed the offense. Think of it like this:

> If a father takes money from his child's piggy bank, nothing is going to happen to that dad.
> If a child takes money from his father's billfold, he might find himself being introduced to Mr. Wooden Spoon.
> If an employee takes money from his boss, he will receive discipline or a pink slip.
> If you don't pay your taxes and, in essence, steal from the government, then say hello to your new bunky, Bubba.

In each instance theft has taken place, yet the punishment for the same crime increases. Why?

While the identical crime was committed, the one against whom the crime was committed was greater or more powerful. Punishment increases for the crime based on the offended party's status.

Now, imagine stealing from the Creator of the universe. Because He is eternal and infinitely great, powerful, holy, righteous, and good, the penalty for any crimes against Him demands an eternal and infinitely awful punishment.

It seems extreme to the atheist, and perhaps to us, that God would say that all liars will have their part in a Lake of Fire (Rev. 21:8). Why would God condemn someone to eternal, conscious torment for a fib? It is not the spectacular nature of the sin per se, but the One against whom the sin is committed.

Furthermore, God hates lying because deceit is contrary to His character and nature. God is truth. He does not write the standard of what is true and false, He *is* the standard of truth and everything else is false. Therefore, God loves what is true and hates what is false.

You Hate Lying, Too

EHarmony.com is the on-line dating service that has 29 "dimensions of compatibility" to match people with similar likes and dislikes. Applicants must take a test to determine the most desirable attributes in a possible mate and the least desirable qualities of a potential spouse. Which characteristics do you suppose is the number one "I can't stand" attribute for both males and females?

> Wrong political party
> Bad manners
> Boring
> Uneducated
> Not ambitious
> Not kind
> Not successful
> Not rich
> Not fashionable

While all of those things are important, the number 1 "I can't stand attribute" is: lying. We hate it when someone lies to us. Why? Because we are image bearers of the One who is Truth. We hate lying because God hates lying.

We also hate lying because it is more than just fibbing, it is a personal slight. It is the liar's way of saying, "I don't respect you." That is precisely what we tell God when we lie. Lying is our special way of saying to God, "I hate the truth. I hate you."

That is just one reason why the Bible calls us "enemies of God" and His wrath abides upon us (Col. 1:21; Rom. 5:10; John 3:20). Humans are not neutral toward their Maker. The Bible is clear: we are haters of God. He is our enemy. We do not love Him, we despise Him.

> The mind set on the flesh is hostile toward God; for it does not subject itself to the law of God, for it is not even able to do so, and those who are in the flesh cannot please God (Rom. 8:7–8).

For everyone who does evil **hates** the Light [Jesus], and does not come to the Light for fear that his deeds will be exposed (John 3:20).

[Jesus said to His disciples,] "If the world **hates** you, you know that it has **hated** Me before it **hated** you (John 15:18).

He who **hates** Me **hates** My Father also. If I had not done among them the works which no one else did, they would not have sin; but now they have both seen and **hated** Me and My Father as well. But they have done this to fulfill the word that is written in their Law, "They **hated** Me without a cause" (John 15:23–25).

You adulteresses, do you not know that friendship with the world is **hostility** toward God? Therefore whoever wishes to be a friend of the world makes himself an **enemy** of God (James 4:4).

George Burns and Morgan Freeman played God and the world adored them. Perhaps that is the way it works in the movies, but the last time God came to this earth, His name was Jesus Christ and we killed Him.

Nobody is ambivalent toward God. We all hate God and we are earning wrath for the day of wrath.

But because of your stubbornness and unrepentant heart you are **storing up wrath for yourself** in the day of wrath and revelation of the righteous judgment of God, who will **render to each person** according to his deeds: to those who by perseverance in doing good seek for glory and honor and immortality, eternal life; but to those who are selfishly ambitious and do not obey the truth, but obey unrighteousness, **wrath and indignation**. There will be **tribulation and distress** for every soul of man who does evil, of the Jew first and also of the Greek, but glory and honor and peace to everyone who does good, to the Jew first and also to the Greek. For there is no partiality with God (Rom. 2:5–11).

When God judges, it is not because He is mean. He does not judge because He is throwing a tantrum. God judges because His nature demands it.

Because God is just, He will not, He CANNOT overlook sin. God is not a squishy, confused, liberal judge who lets guilty criminals go unpunished. God takes sin seriously. God must punish sin. Must.

Humans, while fallen, are like God in this regard. The reason we have justice systems is because we are image bearers of the One who is perfectly just. We have laws, courts, and punishment for criminals because God has laws, courts, and punishment for criminals.

We love justice because God loves justice. God loves justice because He is just.

Left to Ourselves, We Are in Big Trouble

Because of Adam, you and I are conceived in sin (Ps. 51:5), born in sin, and continually sin as easily as we breathe oxygen. You and I must face the justice bench of God. Alone.

Thankfully, God has another attribute: love.

God did not make up the idea of love and then try to personify it. God *is* love.

God's love is not a sentimental, whimsical, emotional love that is based on the attributes of the object of affection. He does not love us because we are loveable; He loves us because He is love (1 John 4:8). He loves because of His character and nature, not ours. He loves us despite who we are, not because of who we are.

God loves us because He loves us.

Are We Valuable?

Humans are not valuable, but we are valued.

While that sounds like a great big downer, being valued is far better than being valuable. You see, if God loves people only because there is something about some humans that He is just nuts about, what if you don't possess that quality? Then God would not love you.

What would happen if you did possess an attribute that God finds loveable, but that attribute fades?

> - If God loves you for your looks, will He not love you when you grow old and saggy?
> - If God loves you for your sense of humor, does He stop loving you when you are not witty?
> - If God loves you for your money, what happens to God's love if you lose your wealth?

God's love for you is not based on you, it is based on Him. That should come as a tremendous relief. You and I change, but God is immutable, His love never changes (Ps. 102:27; Mal. 3:6; James 1:17). While your attitude toward God can wax and wane, God's attitude toward you never changes. If you are in Christ, God loves you as much as He loves His Son. That is a lot.

The Value of a Footstool

What is the value of an object? Whatever someone will pay for it. You can put a million-dollar asking price on your home (unless you are a prosperity preacher, because that would be giving it away), but if nobody will offer more than $250,000, it is only worth a quarter million.

A merchant can put any price tag he wants on his goods, but if nobody buys them, then they are worth nothing. The only value an object has is the value that someone places on it.

You can pick up a brand new footstool at Target for less than a hundred bucks. You could also buy an old, worn-out hassock for hundreds of thousands of dollars. What's the difference? John F. Kennedy used that footstool.

The former president's footstool was worth that much because somebody (with way too much extra cash) paid that much for it. If you brought JFK's ratty footstool to Moldova and tried to sell it, you would get pennies for it. Why? Moldovans don't value JFK's footstool.

The value of an object is not based on the object itself but the value that someone places on it. You and I are dirt and water. And yet, God places His special love on us despite what we are worth. This is what makes God's love exceptional and so amazing.

> [Jesus said,] "For God **so loved the world**, that He gave His only begotten Son, that whoever believes in Him shall not perish, but have eternal life" (John 3:16).

God's Love and Justice Meet

God hates sin because of His righteous nature. God loves us because of His loving nature. These two attributes collided most powerfully in one location: the Cross.

How much does God hate sin? He crushed His own Son. The sinless Son of God was credited with your sin and God poured out His fury on His beloved Son because Jesus had been credited with your sin.

How much does God love you? He crushed His own Son on your behalf that you might be forgiven.

God's wrath and love are most vividly on display at the Cross. If you ever doubt God's settled anger at sin, look at the Cross. If you ever doubt how kind, good, and loving God is, look at the Cross.

Jesus' brutal death on the Cross is God's greatest and clearest demonstration of His wrath and love.

A Shadowy Picture

Over two thousand years before God's wrath and love collided at the Cross, the Bible records a shadowy picture of His anger and mercy: Noah's ark.

The people of Genesis 6 were sinning continually and God's anger reached the point that He determined to destroy the entire world with a flood.

> The LORD said, "I will **blot out** man whom I have created from the face of the land, from man to animals to creeping things and to birds of the sky; for **I am sorry** that I have made them" (Gen. 6:7).

There we see God's anger. Here we see God's kindness:

> Then God said to Noah, "The end of all flesh has come before Me; for the earth is filled with **violence** because of them; and behold, I am about to **destroy** them with the earth. Make for yourself an **ark** of gopher wood; you shall make the ark with rooms, and shall cover it inside and out with **pitch** (Gen. 6:13–14).

God promised to destroy the earth with a flood, but He also provided a way of escape — a great big boat. God commanded Noah to do two things:

1. Build an ark to provide an escape from the waters of judgment.
2. Preach repentance to the "continually evil" sinners.

God didn't just get annoyed one day and open up the floodgates. Instead, He commanded Noah to call men to repentance for 120 years! Now that is patience. That is love.

Success Rate: 0

After 120 years of faithful preaching, Noah had zero converts. Not one person took him up on God's offer to escape the wrath to come by entering the boat. Only Noah, Mrs. Noah, and three little Noahs and their wives entered the boat.

> So they went into the ark to Noah, by twos of all flesh in which was the breath of life. Those that entered, male and female of all flesh, entered as God had commanded him; and **the LORD closed it behind him** (Gen. 7:15–16).

God opened up the heavens and released the fountains of the deep. As promised, God destroyed every human and animal that was not in the ark. But God did not kill everyone; He saved those who believed in Him. It was only eight people, but He still saved people.

God judged the world in righteousness and showed mercy at the same time. The water was God's instrument of judgment; the ark was God's means of rescue.

More than an Ark

The New Testament Book of 1 Peter 3:18–22 tells us that Jesus is like that ark. Noah's ark is a shadowy picture of Jesus and His work on the Cross.

> > The ark saved people from God's judgment; Jesus saves people from God's judgment.
> > Those who were in the ark were spared from death; those who are in Jesus are spared from eternal destruction.
> > The ark saved. Jesus saves.

More than Pitch

God commanded Noah to "cover the ark inside and out with pitch" (Gen. 6:14). The ark was made watertight by covering it internally and externally with this waterproof substance. It is the word "pitch" that leads us again to Jesus.

According to *Strong's Concordance*, the Hebrew word for pitch is *kaphar* and it means "to cover, purge, make an atonement, make reconciliation." *Kaphar* is used 70 times in the Bible to mean "atonement" as it relates to blood sacrifice. Yom Kippur (Day of Atonement) come from the word *kaphar*. There is only one exception to the use of *kaphar*, and it is here in Genesis where it refers to the substance which covers the ark inside and out. *Kaphar* is the word used to describe the pitch used on the ark to keep the waters of judgment out.

In the New Testament, the word for "pitch" is translated "propitiation." The New Testament makes it clear that Jesus is our pitch, He is our propitiation.

And if anyone sins, we have an Advocate with the Father, Jesus Christ the righteous; and He Himself is the **propitiation for our sins**; and not for ours only, but also for those of the whole world (1 John 2:1–2).

In this is love, not that we loved God, but that He loved us and sent His Son to be the **propitiation for our sins** (1 John 4:10).

Jesus is the pitch that saves us from God's judgment.

More than a Door

The ark was a humongous boat. For such a large vessel, you would think there would be multiple doors, but the ark had only one door. To have only one door for such a big boat is remarkable, but we see the significance in "only one door" when Jesus announced,

> I am the **door**; if anyone enters **through Me**, he will be **saved** (John 10:9).

Just as the ark of salvation had only one door, there is only one entrance into eternal salvation. Jesus is the "one door" that we must enter to have eternal life. There are not multiple doors. You cannot create your own door. Sincerity in other doors will not help on the Day of Judgment. We must enter the ark of safety through the only door that actually exists, Jesus Christ.

Jesus Is Our Ark

> Jesus is the ark of our salvation.
> Jesus is our propitiation, our atonement, the "pitch" who appeases the wrath of God and saves us from the judgment to come.
> Jesus is the only door that we must enter if we will be saved.

The story of Noah's ark is indeed a story about God's judgment on mankind. Far more than that, we see a picture of God's kindness in providing a rescuer for us: Jesus Christ, the ark of our salvation.

How Great Is God's Love?

How would you treat people who continually hated you? What would you do to someone who persistently, willfully, aggressively despised you?

Think of your dog. How long would you tolerate your hound if he repeatedly bit your hand every time you fed him? When would you send your pooch packing for constantly chewing on your shoes? How many times would your dog have to soil your carpets before you found a vet to administer a special shot?

You and I are worse than dogs. Dogs don't have consciences; we do. Dogs don't know better, but we do.

The people in the day of Noah were evil continually and yet, God provided a means of salvation for those who hate Him. That is amazing grace.

God's forbearance is beyond our comprehension. Day after day, minute by minute we ignore Him. Years of non-stop blessings are delivered to us from His gracious hand and we refuse to thank Him. Decades of free air, free food, free shelter, free everything. How do we repay Him? We hate Him.

And yet God sends us an ark.

Instead of pouring out His wrath, He provides a vehicle of rescue. Instead of destroying us for our sins, He crushed His own Son on our behalf. Instead of obliterating us, He preaches to us, "Run to the ark. Run through the Door. Run to Jesus and be saved from the wrath that is to come."

250

A.D. 33: Jesus crucified
A.D. 30: Jesus begins ministry
A.D. 26: John the Baptist begins preaching

0 — 0: Jesus is born

397–5 B.C.: The silent years

250

397 B.C.: Malachi is Israel's last prophet until John the Baptist
500 — 515 B.C.: Jerusalem rebuilt and temple completed
536 B.C.: Jews start returning to Jerusalem
586 B.C.: Southern Kingdom falls to Babylon
721 B.C.: Northern Kingdom falls to Assyria
750

975 B.C.: Israel split in two

1000 — 1004 B.C.: Solomon's temple completed
1015 B.C.: Solomon becomes king
1055 B.C.: David becomes king

1250

1451 B.C.: The Jews enter the Promised Land
1491–1451 B.C.: The Jews wander the desert
1500 — 1491 B.C.: Moses leads the Exodus out of Egypt

1700–1574 B.C.: Joseph and his brothers have lots of babies
1750 — 1739 B.C.: Joseph sold into slavery in Egypt

1836 B.C.: Jacob born

1896 B.C.: Isaac born

2000 — 1996 B.C. Abraham born

2250

2349 B.C.: Noah and the Global Flood
2500

2750

3000

3250

Timeline
4004 B.C. — A.D. 33

3500

3750

4000

4004 B.C.: Creation, Adam and Eve, Cain and Abel

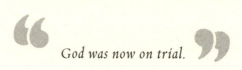
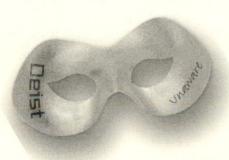

Chapter Seven

Jesus Is the Rock

No, Jesus is not Dwayne Johnson. Jesus is a much better rock.

A Covenant Promise

It is the 21st century B.C., four centuries after the Flood. God appeared to a man named Abraham and cut an irrevocable covenant (contract) with him. God promised Abraham that He would provide a land (Israel), a nation (the Jewish people) and a seed (Jesus Christ) (Gen. 17).

The rest of the Bible is the story of God making good on that promise. He allowed old Abraham to have children who would become the Jewish people who would dwell in the land of Israel and produce a special seed, a Messiah.

> Now the promises were spoken to Abraham and to his **seed**. He does not say, "And to seeds," as referring to many, but rather to one, "And to your **seed**," that is, **Christ** (Gal. 3:16).

Supernatural Proof

Israel is the Promised Land because it is — you guessed it — land promised by God. If you want supernatural proof that God exists, consider the Jewish people and the land of Israel.

In A.D. 135, the Romans booted the Jews out of the land of Israel. The Jews did not return to live in the Promised Land until 1948. For 18 centuries, the Jews were without a homeland, yet they remained a people. No nation has ever survived without a homeland for more than a few generations. It is a miracle that the Jews remained a people for over eighteen hundred years as a disbursed people. That is a good old-fashioned miracle.

Have you ever met a Hittite, Girgashite, Amorite, Canaanite, Perizzite, Hivite, or Jebusite? Nope. Those nations disappeared when they were invaded and lost control of their land. Yet the Jews remain a people despite the fact that they were without a homeland for centuries. Why? Because God promised Abraham that there would always be a land, nation and a seed.

Making Babies

God gave Abraham this three-fold promise despite the fact that Abraham was beyond childbearing years and the land was occupied by pagan nations. God was faithful to His word and miraculously gave Abraham a son (Isaac) who had a son (Jacob) who had 12 sons, including a boy named Donny Osmond, aka, Joseph.

Joseph's 11 brothers were a tad jealous of their braggart brother and they dumped him into a well and told their dear ol' dad (Jacob) that Joseph, his favorite, was dead. With brothers like that, who needs sisters?

Joseph was rescued out of the well and brought to Egypt where he was tossed into a jail, interpreted some dreams and became Pharaoh's right-hand man. Because of Joseph's ability to interpret dreams, he informed Pharaoh that a famine was on the way and he encouraged the Grand Poobah to store up grain for the coming food shortage. Pharaoh thought Joseph was pretty nifty, so he made the Dream Interpreter his right-hand man.

In the meantime, the famine hit the land where Joseph's brothers were living and they skedaddled to Egypt to find some food. Surprise — they appeared before their brother, Joseph, and a tearful reunion ensued.

The brothers stayed in Egypt with Joseph and got busy making babies. Lots and lots of babies. No, seriously, like, homeschool family amounts of babies. As the years rolled on, Joseph, the brothers, and the friendly pharaoh died, leaving the Jewish people in Egypt under a not-so-nice pharaoh who enslaved them.

That is how the Jews ended up as slaves in Egypt for four hundred years. For the next four centuries the Jews worked and multiplied. A lot.

The next time you hear someone complain about the minimum wage, just remind them of the Jewish wages in Egypt: nothing. Four centuries of harsh labor, squalid conditions, and frustration. The heart cry of the enslaved Jews had to have been, "When will God make good on His covenant promise to Abraham and give us a land?"

Finally, God sent the Jews a deliverer named Charlton Heston who led the children of Israel into the Promised Land.

Unfortunately, the journey was a bit of a nightmare. The Jews had a tendency to complain about their circumstances and they lacked faith that God would indeed bring them to the Promised Land. That brings us to the wilderness and a jaw-dropping courtroom drama.

A Wilderness Courtroom Drama

The Jews just crossed through the Red Sea, courtesy of a pretty impressive miracle. God parted the water and brought the Jews through the sea while drowning the bad guys. Top that, Hollywood!

> Then Moses led Israel from the Red Sea, and they went out into the wilderness of Shur; and they went three days in the wilderness and found **no water**. When they came to Marah, they could **not drink** the waters of Marah, for they were **bitter**; therefore it was named Marah. So the people **grumbled** at Moses, saying, "What shall we drink?"

> Then he cried out to the LORD, and the LORD showed him a tree; and he threw it into the waters, and the **waters became sweet** (Exod. 15:22–25).

The Jews had just witnessed ten nasty plagues, a Red Sea parting, and bitter water turned into Perrier. The very next scene in the Bible shows God providing bread and meat for them in the wilderness. You would think the Jews would have enough evidence to believe that God was going to take care of them. You would think.

Short-term Memory

Unfortunately, the Jewish people failed to remember the miracles that God had performed for their deliverance.

> Then all the congregation of the sons of Israel journeyed by stages from the **wilderness** of Sin, according to the command of the LORD, and camped at Rephidim, and there was **no water** for the people to drink. Therefore the people **quarreled with Moses** and said, "Give us water that we may drink" (Exod. 17:1–2).

Seriously? Just two chapters earlier God provided the Jews with water and here they are, quarreling with Moses about water.

> And Moses said to them, "Why do you quarrel with me? Why do **you test the LORD?**" But the people thirsted there for water; and they **grumbled** against Moses and said, "Why, now, have you brought us up from Egypt, to kill us and our children and our live-stock with thirst?" So Moses cried out to the LORD, saying, "What shall I do to this people? A little more and **they will stone me**" (Exod. 17:2–4).

The Hebrew word for "quarrel" is the root of *meribah*, meaning, they "lodged a formal complaint" against Moses. This was a legal term. Israel was filing a lawsuit against Moses.

Moses was no dummy. As God's representative to the people, Moses realized that their lawsuit was actually against God Himself (Exod. 17:2). God was now on trial.

A Courtroom Drama

> Then the LORD said to Moses, "**Pass before** the people and take with you some of the **elders** of Israel; and take in your hand your **staff** with which you struck the Nile, and go. Behold, **I will stand before you** there on the **rock** at Horeb" (Exod. 17:5–6).

Due to the extreme seriousness of the accusation, God formalized their accusations and created a courtroom. God instructed Moses to stand before the accusers with other elders to serve as the judges and witnesses of this lawsuit.

Moses' staff plays no small role in this scene. The staff was Moses' symbol of authority to make a judgment and pass sentence. This was the staff of judgment God gave Moses to execute justice with Pharaoh.

In Israel, a guilty criminal would be placed before the judge who would use his rod to administer justice on the guilty criminal (Deut. 25:1–3). Here, God submitted Himself to be punished by the very same rod.

In the Old Testament, the accused would stand before God's representative. Now God stood accused before a human court. God stood on the rock awaiting judgment from His guilty accusers. This is a shocking scene.

God permitted the criminals to place Him, the judge of the universe, on trial. The Creator allowed His creation to pass sentence and execute judgment on Him with the rod of judgment. God, the innocent One, stands in the place of the guilty ones.

We now witness one of the most staggering scenes in the entire Old Testament as God continued His instructions to Moses:

> ". . . and you shall **strike the rock**, and water will come out of it, that the people may drink." And Moses did so in the sight of the elders of Israel (Exod. 17:6).

Dr. Edmund Clowney describes the event:

> Before the face of Moses the judge, with his rod uplifted, stands the God of Israel. The Lord stands in the prisoners dock. Moses cannot strike into the heart of God's shekinah glory. God commands He strike the rock.
>
> God, the Rock, identifies Himself with the rock by standing on it. God stands in the place of the accused, and the penalty of the judgment is inflicted.
>
> Is God, then, guilty? No, it is the people who are guilty. In rebellion they have refused to trust the faithfulness of God. Yet God, the Judge, bears the judgment; He receives the blow that their rebellion deserves. The law must be satisfied: if God's people are to be spared, He must bear their punishment.[1]

And Who Is That Rock?

Fifteen hundred years after this wilderness courtroom drama, the Apostle Paul tells us who the Rock was.

> For I do not want you to be unaware, brethren, that our fathers were all under the cloud and all passed through the [Red] sea; and all were baptized into Moses in the cloud and in the sea; and all ate the same spiritual food; and all drank the same spiritual drink, for

---

1. Much gratitude to the late Dr. Edmund Clowney for his judicial understanding of the scene at Meribah. Edmund Clowney, *The Unfolding Mystery: Discovering Christ in the Old Testament* (Phillipsburg, NJ: P&R Pub., 2013).

they were drinking from a **spiritual rock** which followed them; and
the rock was Christ (1 Cor. 10:1–4).

Jesus Christ is the rock!

Jesus Christ, the righteous one, stands in the place of guilty people and
receives the punishment they deserve. Jesus, the innocent, stands in the
place of His guilty accusers that they might be found innocent. Jesus, the
Just, was treated as if He were unjust so the unjust ones could be made just.

Jesus was placed on trial by guilty people, sentenced by guilty people,
executed by guilty people, to redeem guilty people. The trial at Meribah was
a picture of the trial of Jesus Christ.

> > God was falsely accused. Jesus was falsely accused.
> > God stood on trial before men. Jesus stood on trial before men.
> > God stood in the place of men. Jesus stood in the place of men.
> > God was stricken. Jesus stricken, smitten, and afflicted.
> > God, the innocent, paid the fine for the guilty. Jesus, who knew
> >   no sin, was made to be sin that we might be made the righ-
> >   teousness of God (2 Cor. 5:21).

Before the Jews were allowed to enter the Promised Land, God gave them
another picture of the gospel. God showed them that guilty people need
Him to pay the fine for their lawbreaking.

Most of the Jews failed to grasp this, and they continually attempted to
satisfy the justice of God through their self-righteous efforts. They missed
the gospel. They missed grace.

Have you?

> *Jesus is the spiritual water that if consumed one time offers eternal life.*

Chapter Eight

Jesus Is the Living Water

Not only was Jesus the rock who stood in our place to take the punishment we deserve, He is also the life-giving water that flowed from the rock.

There came a woman of Samaria to draw water. Jesus said to her, "Give Me a drink." For His disciples had gone away into the city to buy food. Therefore the Samaritan woman said to Him, "How is it that You, being a Jew, ask me for a drink since I am a Samaritan woman?" (For Jews have no dealings with Samaritans.)

Jesus answered and said to her, "If you knew the gift of God, and who it is who says to you, 'Give Me a drink,' you would have asked Him, and He would have given you **living water**."

She said to Him, "Sir, You have nothing to draw with and the well is deep; where then do You get that **living water**? You are not greater than our father Jacob, are You, who gave us the well, and drank of it himself and his sons and his cattle?"

Jesus answered and said to her, "Everyone who drinks of this water will thirst again; but whoever drinks of the water that I will give him shall **never thirst**; but the water that I will give him will become in him a well of water springing up to eternal life" (John 4:7–14).

What Is He Talking About?

Jesus was doing two things here; first, He was calling Himself the *living* water. Physical water requires constant consumption for physical life. Jesus is the spiritual water that if consumed one time offers eternal life.

Second, Jesus was alluding to the prophet Jeremiah, who spoke for God over 600 years earlier.

> For My people have committed two evils:
> They have forsaken Me,
> The fountain of **living waters**,
> To hew for themselves cisterns,
> Broken cisterns
> That can hold no water (Jer. 2:13).

By alluding to God's words in Jeremiah, not only was Jesus equating Himself with God, the living water, but He was also teaching that His offer of spiritual life is a free gift. Cisterns were man-made reservoirs to catch and store rainwater. Cisterns are deficient for three reasons:

1. They leak.
2. The water that is captured and stored is often dirty and lukewarm.
3. They contain a limited amount of water.

On the other hand, an underground well (living water) provides fresh water: cool, clean, refreshing, limitless.

What was Jesus saying? "Stop trying to quench your spiritual thirst with your broken, man-made efforts that cannot satisfy. Instead, come to Me for free, living water and you will never thirst. You will never die."

Staggering Symbolism

Jesus made the same offer of life-giving water to everyone when He preached at the Old Testament Festival of Booths in Jerusalem. The fall Festival of Booths was a major celebration. All Jews were required to attend this festival to give thanks for seven days and remember God's deliverance of His people. Jerusalem was packed.

On the seventh day of the feast, the temple priests would march to the pool of Siloam and walk around the temple seven times and quote the prophet Isaiah.

> Then you will say **on that day**,
> "I will give thanks to You, O LORD;
> For although You were angry with me,
> **Your anger is turned away**,
> And You comfort me.
> "Behold, God is **my salvation**,
> I will trust and not be afraid;
> For the LORD GOD is my strength and song,
> And He has become **my salvation**."
> Therefore you will joyously draw **water**
> From the **springs of salvation** (Isa. 12:1–3).

Hundreds of thousands of people shouted for joy while the priests carried water around the temple while thanking God for deliverance. It is at that moment when Jesus lifted up His voice and shouted, "If anyone is thirsty, let him **come to Me** and drink!" (John 7:37).

One wonders if anyone understood exactly what Jesus was saying. One wonders if anyone remembered the next three verses of Isaiah chapter 12.

> And **in that day** you will say, "Give thanks to the LORD, call on His name. Make known His deeds among the peoples; Make them remember that His name is exalted." Praise the LORD in song, for He has done excellent things; Let this be known throughout the earth. Cry aloud and **shout for joy**, O inhabitant of [Jerusalem], For **great in your midst is the Holy One of Israel** (Isa. 12:4–6).

The people shouted for joy, and yet His own did not recognize Him as their source of joy (John 1:10). God's people did not realize that in that moment, the promise of Isaiah was being fulfilled. Jesus, the Holy One of Israel, was in their midst.

Another Old Testament Allusion

Jesus regularly made references to the Old Testament when He preached and spoke. When He shouted to the people to quench their spiritual thirst in Him, Jesus was no doubt alluding to Isaiah chapter 55, where God spoke to the Jews through His prophet Isaiah.

> Ho! Every one who thirsts, **come to the waters**;
> And you who have **no money** come, buy and eat.
> Come, buy wine and milk
> Without money and **without cost**.
> Why do you spend money for what is not bread,
> And your wages for what does not satisfy? (Isa. 55:1–2).

Jesus offered Himself as the free living water who grants everlasting life. No cost. No charge. Free.

What Will You Do with His Offer?

Are you still trying to please God with your own works? Isaiah makes it clear, your efforts cannot purchase what you need. You need living water. You need Jesus.

What should you do if you now desire God's free gift of everlasting life purchased by the Living Water, Jesus Christ? You should do the same thing that Isaiah told the work-righteous Jews to do in Isaiah 55.

> Seek the LORD while He may be found;
> **Call upon Him** while He is near.
> Let the wicked **forsake** his way
> And the unrighteous man his thoughts;
> And let him **return** to the LORD,
> And He will have compassion on him,
> And to our God,
> For He will **abundantly pardon** (Isa. 55:6–7).

What must you do to inherit eternal life? Repent and place your faith in the Living Water, the Lord Jesus Christ.

250	
	A.D. 33: Jesus crucified
	A.D. 30: Jesus begins ministry
	A.D. 26: John the Baptist begins preaching
0	0: Jesus is born
	397–5 B.C.: The silent years
250	
	397 B.C.: Malachi is Israel's last prophet until John the Baptist
500	515 B.C.: Jerusalem rebuilt and temple completed
	536 B.C.: Jews start returning to Jerusalem
	586 B.C.: Southern Kingdom falls to Babylon
750	721 B.C.: Northern Kingdom falls to Assyria
	975 B.C.: Israel split in two
1000	1004 B.C.: Solomon's temple completed
	1015 B.C.: Solomon becomes king
	1055 B.C.: David becomes king
1250	
	1451 B.C.: The Jews enter the Promised Land
	1491–1451 B.C.: The Jews wander the desert
1500	1491 B.C.: Moses leads the Exodus out of Egypt
	1700–1574 B.C.: Joseph and his brothers have lots of babies
	1739 B.C.: Joseph sold into slavery in Egypt
1750	
	1836 B.C.: Jacob born
	1896 B.C.: Isaac born
2000	1996 B.C. Abraham born
2250	
	2349 B.C.: Noah and the Global Flood
2500	
2750	
3000	
3250	

Timeline

4004 B.C. – A.D. 33

3500	
3750	
4000	
	4004 B.C.: Creation, Adam and Eve, Cain and Abel

> *The murmuring Jews whined about God's provision for them,*
> *but instead of giving them wrath, God gave them bread.*

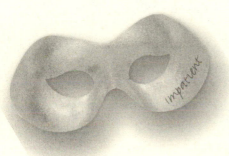

Chapter 9

Jesus Is the Bread

The grass is always greener on the other side, isn't it? That cliché isn't true just for horses, it is true for us.

> > The weather was better yesterday.
> > I like our old house better.
> > If I get that job, then I'll be happy.
> > My mother's cooking was better than your cooking (a sentence, if uttered, you will wish you could take back).

Grumbling Again

In between the two water episodes at Masah (Exodus 15) and Meribah (Exodus 17), the Jews were busy complaining. Again.

> Then they set out from Elim, and all the congregation of the sons of Israel came to the wilderness of Sin, which is between Elim and Sinai, on the fifteenth day of the second month after their departure from the land of Egypt. The whole congregation of the sons of Israel

grumbled against Moses and Aaron in the wilderness. The sons of
Israel said to them, "Would that we had died by the LORD's hand
in the land of Egypt, when we sat by the pots of meat, when we ate
bread to the full; for you have brought us out into this wilderness to
kill this whole assembly with **hunger**" (Exod. 16:1–3).

Just like us, the wandering Jews thought the grass was greener back in Egypt.
Fascinating. They were slaves in Egypt, but they preferred the bondage of
Egypt to the freedom of the wilderness because they missed meat. Was slav-
ery in Egypt with meat better than freedom in the wilderness without meat?
Of course not, but that is the way it is when we are not content; everything
else seems better.

In Egypt, the Jews were slaves without a union representative. They
worked long days for nothing, but received all the lashes they wanted. Or
didn't want. Long days making bricks is not a glamour gig. Slave labor is
hardly something to long for, but the Jews believed their stomachs were
more important than their backs. The Jews complained about Wilderness
food versus Slave food.

Why Is Complaining Bad?

God is the sovereign provider of everything that we have (Ps. 145:15). When
we complain, we are basically saying:

> > You are doing a lousy job, God.
> > You don't know what You are doing, God.
> > You should do more for me, God.
> > I could provide better than You, God.

It is shocking that God doesn't zap complainers on the spot.

What Would You Have Done?

God sent ten plagues to force Pharaoh to release His children. God parted
a Red Sea on their behalf. God produced pure water from a rock. And yet,
they grumbled. How would you have treated the malcontents? We can only
imagine how we would have responded to their grumbling.

What God Did

Then the LORD said to Moses, "Behold, I will rain **bread** from
heaven for you" (Exod. 16:4).

You and I would have clobbered the complainers; God showed them kindness. You and I would have acted like an angry dictator; God acted like a caterer.

God Is Way Patient

It is not uncommon for unbelievers to think God was "mean" in the Old Testament. The atheist will cite God's slaughter of the Caananites who lived in the Promised Land that God gave to the Jews. Atheists complain that God should not have killed all of the Caananites just for living in the wrong place at the wrong time. That is hardly an accurate picture of what happened.

God promised Abraham a land, nation, and seed. God waited four hundred years before He executed judgment on the pagan Caananites and allowed the Jews to move into the Promised Land flowing with milk and honey.

Do you remember what was going on in the Promised Land during those four centuries? The pagans were acting like pagans. Worshipers of Molech placed their own babies onto the scalding hot arms of their man-made idol. Imagine that — cruel, painful, torturous baby sacrifices, and yet, God was patient for four hundred years before He wiped them out. He is hardly capricious.

God is never mean. In fact, God is exceedingly long-suffering and amazingly kind. The murmuring Jews whined about God's provision for them, but instead of giving them wrath, God gave them bread.

Fast-forward 1,500 Years

Jesus had just performed another miracle. He graciously fed five thousand men, plus women and children, near the Sea of Galilee. Were the people satisfied with the bread He provided?

> So they said to Him, "What then do You do for a sign, so that we may see, and believe You? **What work** do You perform? Our fathers ate the **manna** in the wilderness; as it is written, 'He gave them bread out of heaven to eat' " (John 6:30–31).

Say what? Jesus provided a free lunch of bread and fish for over 10,000 people, and how did the freeloaders respond? They asked Jesus for a miracle. If this were a cartoon, an anvil would have fallen on their collective noggins.

The next time an unbeliever tells you they would believe in God "if He would just do a miracle," you will know that is not true. Miracles do not convert people, God converts people.

Whoomp, There It Is!

The manna/bread that God graciously provided for the complaining Jews in the wilderness was actually a picture of Jesus, the Bread of Life.

> Jesus then said to them, "Truly, truly, I say to you, it is not Moses who has given you the **bread out of heaven**, but it is My Father who gives you the true bread out of heaven. For the bread of God is that which comes down out of heaven, and gives life to the world."
>
> Then they said to Him, "Lord, always give us this bread."
>
> Jesus said to them, "I **am the bread of life**; he who comes to Me will **not hunger**, and he who believes in Me will **never thirst** (John 6:32–35).

The bread that God provided the Jews in the wilderness was actual bread, but it was also a picture of a better bread — Jesus, the Bread of Life.

Talk about amazing grace! The wandering Jews complained and God gave them manna. We complain and He provides us with spiritual Bread, His own beloved Son.

Jesus Christ, the Bread of Life, is offered freely to complainers who deserve an eternity of hunger pains. Jesus offers Himself as a Living Bread so that we will never hunger in hell.

Are You a Complainer?

Who of us doesn't complain?

> I NEED a new car.
> I NEED new clothes.
> I HATE this house.
> I HATE this food.

Just like the grumbling Jews in the wilderness, you and I complain. Constantly.

> I don't like this.
> I don't like that.
> I don't want to go here.
> I don't want to go there.
> I can't stand this.
> I can't stand that.

How God Responds to Our Complaining

Our complaining insults God and He offers us the Bread from Heaven.

Our murmuring offends God and He gives us His Son.

Our whining is an affront to God and He provides the food that forever satisfies.

You Have Eaten This Bread

If you have tasted the goodness of God and believed on His Son, then you know that nothing satisfies like He does. You know that the Bread of Life is better than any physical provision.

You have been pardoned and purchased by the King. Despite your grumbling, complaining, and whining, God loved you by providing for your vast spiritual need. What a God!

You Have Not Eaten This Bread

You have not partaken of the Bread of Life and now you realize that you are starving. What should you do? You should do what Jesus instructed the ungrateful beneficiaries of His free fish lunch to do.

> Truly, truly, I say to you, he who believes has **eternal life**. I am the **bread of life**. Your fathers ate the manna in the wilderness, and **they died**. This is the bread which comes down out of heaven, so that one may eat of it and **not die**. I am the **living bread** that came down out of heaven; if anyone eats of this bread, he will **live forever** (John 6:47–51).

What are you waiting for? Why would you starve to death?

> O **taste** and see that the LORD is good; How blessed is the man who takes refuge **in Him!** (Ps. 34:8).

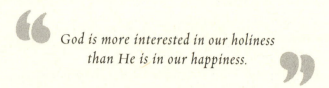

God is more interested in our holiness than He is in our happiness.

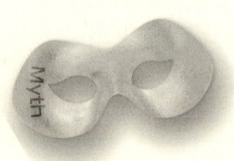

Myth

Chapter 10

Jesus Is the Bronze Serpent

You guessed it. The Jews are still wandering around the wilderness waiting for God to give them the green light to go into the Promised Land.

You guessed it again. They are complaining about food. Again.

> Then they set out from Mount Hor by the way of the Red Sea, to go around the land of Edom; and the people became **impatient** because of the journey. The people spoke against God and Moses, "**Why** have you brought us up out of Egypt to die in the wilderness? For there is no food and no water, and we **loathe** this **miserable** food" (Num. 21:4–5).

You are probably thinking, "God's going to be nice to them again." You are now three for three!

> The LORD sent **fiery serpents** among the people and they bit the people, so that many people of Israel died (Num. 21:6).

How Is That Being Nice?

How is sending fiery serpents kind? Well, humans can have thick skulls sometimes. We can be slow learners. Because of our slowness to learn, God, in His kindness, will do whatever is necessary for us to learn important things (Heb. 12:6; Prov. 3:12; Rev. 3:19).

God permits or plans pain to move us toward perfection. Sometimes God sends or allows hardship to lead us to repentance. That is precisely what God did for the Jews by sending a bunch of poisonous snakes.

> So the people came to Moses and said, "**We have sinned**, because we have spoken against the LORD and you; intercede with the LORD, that He may remove the serpents from us." And Moses interceded for the people (Num. 21:7).

The Jews sinned, God sent a calamity, the Jews repented. They learned their lesson fast, but they still needed an antidote for the poisonous sting of the cursed serpents.

God's Remedy for the Sting of Death

> Then the LORD said to Moses, "Make a **fiery serpent**, and set it on a standard [pole]; and it shall come about, that everyone who is bitten, when he looks at it, he will **live**."
> And Moses made a **bronze serpent** and set it on the standard; and it came about, that if a serpent bit any man, when he **looked** to the bronze serpent, he **lived** (Num. 21:8–9).

Once again, God provided forgiveness and provision for sinners. God made a way for sinful man to live. To avoid death by snakebite, the bitten Jews were to look toward a bronze serpent.

> The bronze serpent was lifted up on a pole.
> The bronze serpent represented the curse.
> The bronze serpent provided life to those who looked toward it.

There He Is Again

Jesus said,

> "As Moses **lifted up the serpent** in the wilderness, even so must the **Son of Man be lifted up**; so that **whoever believes** will in Him have **eternal life**" (John 3:14–15).

"For God so loved the world, that He gave His only begotten Son, that whoever believes in Him shall not perish, but have eternal life" (John 3:16).

Jesus Christ, God's perfect sacrifice for sin, is the bronze serpent in the wilderness.

> Just as the bronze serpent was lifted on a pole, Jesus was lifted up on a Cross.
> Just as the bronze serpent represented the Curse, Jesus became a curse for us.
> Just as those who would look to the bronze serpent and live, if we will look to Jesus, we too will live.

Christ redeemed us from the curse of the Law, having become a curse for us — for it is written, "**Cursed** is everyone who **hangs on a tree**" — in order that in Christ Jesus the blessing of Abraham might come to the Gentiles, so that we would receive the promise of the Spirit through faith (Gal. 3:13–14).

Did God really send snakes to the grumbling Jews in the wilderness? Yes. Did some of them really get bitten? Yes. Did Moses really lift a bronze serpent on a pole? Yes. Did the bitten Jews who looked to the serpent live? Yes.

Those events actually happened, but those events were merely a fuzzy shadow of a greater fulfillment. The bronze serpent was a type of Jesus.

Once again, we see a vivid picture of the crucifixion of Jesus in an Old Testament type that actually occurred almost fifteen hundred years before He was crucified for sinners. That is not luck. That is another demonstration of God's providential power on display.

Does God Still Send Serpents?

Despite the fact that God has given us a manual for living, we can be just like the Jews in the wilderness: obstinate (Isa. 65:2). And just like the Jews in the wilderness, God still sends fiery serpents to lead us to repentance.

Never forget, God is more interested in our holiness than He is in our happiness. The next time you feel the sting of God's correction, ask yourself the question, "Of what do I need to repent?" When you do, God will forgive. That is the way He is.

You Have Looked at Jesus on the Cross

If you have seen and responded to what Jesus has done for you on the Cross, then you have been made the "righteousness of God."

> He made Him who **knew no sin** to be sin on our behalf, so that
> we might become the **righteousness of God** in Him (2 Cor. 5:21).

You have recognized that the sting of death is the consequence of your sin (Ezek. 18:4). You have seen that Jesus acted as your sin bearer and was lifted onto a pole as your representative. You have received His great love for you.

If you have repented and trusted in Jesus, then you are the beneficiary of a theology called "double imputation."

> Your sins have been credited (imputed) to Jesus.
> Jesus' righteousness has been credited (imputed) to you.

Because of the doctrine of double imputation, not only are you seen as forgiven, but you are actually righteous.

Passive and Active Obedience

Jesus passive obedience was seen when He volunteered to be beaten and crucified at the hands of men as the payment for our sins. Because of Jesus' passive obedience, your sin debt has been brought to zero. Your debt with God has been paid.

Jesus' active obedience was seen when He kept each and every law, thus fulfilling all righteousness (Matt. 3:15). He never did anything wrong.

> Jesus never shaded the truth.
> Jesus never used God's name as a curse word.
> Jesus never had fantasies about women.
> Jesus was never coarse or profane.
> Jesus never said, "I wish I had one of those."
> Jesus never yelled at anyone in anger.

Not only did Jesus never do anything wrong (sins of commission), He never failed to do what was right (sins of omission).

> Jesus always volunteered to help.
> Jesus always encouraged.
> Jesus always went the extra mile.
> Jesus always loved people.

> Jesus always spoke the truth.
> Jesus always gave sacrificially.

All of Jesus' good deeds and righteous behavior have been credited to your account. Jesus' passive obedience brought your account to zero, but Jesus also deposits His righteousness into your account so that you can be seen not just "not guilty," but as righteous.

An Analogy

Think of it this way, if you stood before a judge with a long rap sheet and someone you don't even know stepped into the courtroom and paid your fine, you would be found not guilty. That would be good news indeed.

Now, imagine that stranger never broke a law and had a long résumé of good civic deeds to his credit. What if that stranger asked the judge to have all of his good deeds credited to your account. Not only would you be seen as not guilty, your file would be labeled, "Perfect Citizen."

That is what Jesus does for those who repent and trust in Him.

Another Analogy

You are in debt to the tune of $300,000. The creditors are at your door.

Out of the blue, a stranger appears with a suitcase full of cash and offers the luggage to the creditors on your behalf. You are off the hook.

How much was in the suitcase?

A gazillion dollars.

Your fine is paid, your bank account is filled and your FICO credit score goes from minus five hundred to eight hundred and fifty.

That is what Jesus does for believers. His passive obedience pays the fine while His active obedience puts money into our account. Christians are not simply seen as forgiven, but righteous. When God pulls up your account, He forever sees Jesus' balance.

On the Cross, God looked at Jesus as if He were you, and now He looks at you as if you are Jesus. Because you have looked to Jesus, the curse on a pole, you are His and He is yours.

You Have Not Looked at Jesus on the Cross

Can't you see how consistent and supernatural the Bible is? Can't you see that it is impossible for men to fabricate a story like this? Can't you see that you have been bitten by sin and you are going to die? Can't you see God's provision hanging on a tree? Can't you see God's great love for you?

See how **great a love** the Father has bestowed on us, that we would be called children of God (1 John 3:1).

We know love by this, that He **laid down His life** for us (1 John 3:16).

By this the love of God was manifested in us, that God has sent His only begotten Son into the world so that we might **live through Him**. In this is love, not that we loved God, but that **He loved us** and sent His Son to be the propitiation for our sins (1 John 4:9–10).

Look at the Cross. See the mangled Son of God hanging there. For you. Look. And live.

250

A.D. 33: Jesus crucified
A.D. 30: Jesus begins ministry
A.D. 26: John the Baptist begins preaching

0 — 0: Jesus is born

397–5 B.C.: The silent years

250

397 B.C.: Malachi is Israel's last prophet until John the Baptist
500 — 515 B.C.: Jerusalem rebuilt and temple completed
536 B.C.: Jews start returning to Jerusalem
586 B.C.: Southern Kingdom falls to Babylon

750 — 721 B.C.: Northern Kingdom falls to Assyria

975 B.C.: Israel split in two

1000 — 1004 B.C.: Solomon's temple completed
1015 B.C.: Solomon becomes king
1055 B.C.: David becomes king

1250

1451 B.C.: The Jews enter the Promised Land
1491–1451 B.C.: The Jews wander the desert
1500 — 1491 B.C.: Moses leads the Exodus out of Egypt

1700–1574 B.C.: Joseph and his brothers have lots of babies
1739 B.C.: Joseph sold into slavery in Egypt
1750 —
1836 B.C.: Jacob born

1896 B.C.: Isaac born
2000 — 1996 B.C. Abraham born

2250

2349 B.C.: Noah and the Global Flood
2500

2750

3000

3250

3500

3750

4000

4004 B.C.: Creation, Adam and Eve, Cain and Abel

Timeline
4004 B.C. — A.D. 33

> *What was once a shadowy picture of God dwelling with His people became a Technicolor reality when Jesus came.*

Chapter 11

Jesus Is the Tabernacle

Imagine a pastor who zip-lined onto the platform of his church to begin his sermon.

Picture a pastor who placed his bed on the top of his church and laid in it with his wife for 72 hours to encourage married couples in his congregation to be intimate every day for a month.

Envision a youth pastor who put peanut butter under his armpits and had his students lick it off.

Unfortunately, you don't have to imagine any of those ridiculous scenarios as each of them is, tragically, a reality. Visit YouTube and you can verify this for yourself.

As disgusting, lame, sad, juvenile, pathetic, ridiculous and sordid as those scenarios are, the true tragedy is that most people in today's evangelical churches are being fed pabulum and shenanigans when they could be feasting on what you are about to consume.

Prepare for a banquet. Prepare to see the brilliance, coherence, and supernatural nature of the Bible displayed in HD.

The Bible

The Bible is one book divided into two major sections, the Old and New Testaments. A testament is the writing down of a contract, or covenant, between two parties. The Old Testament records the old covenant and the New Testament records the new covenant. Each Testament focuses on a different covenant, but that does not mean they have nothing in common.

The Old Testament details a number of covenants: Noahic, Abrahamic, Davidic and mostly, the Mosaic covenant. This is the covenant we typically call the old covenant or the Law. The Mosaic covenant was given by God to Moses while he and the Jews were forced to wander around the wilderness.

The old covenant was given to Moses as a "quid-pro-quo contract" between God and His people. If the Jews were obedient, God would bless them; if the Jews were naughty, God would curse them (Deut. 28). Unfortunately, the Jews were persistently unfaithful and disobedient.

When you read about the Jews being taken into captivity by another nation, it is because God promised that would happen if the Jews broke the Mosaic covenant. Every time God returned them back to the land of Israel, it was because God was being faithful to the Abrahamic covenant promise of a land, nation, and seed.

Most of the Old Testament is a two-thousand-year history of Jewish rebellion and God's faithfulness in punishing and restoring them. All of this was done to fulfill the Abrahamic covenant of a land, nation, and seed.

What Is a Covenant?

When you think covenant, think contract. Think of a mutual agreement between two parties who mutually agree to the terms of the covenant. Today's contracts set forth the terms and the penalties for violating the agreement; Old Testament covenants were similar but they were far more profound than a modern contract.

> Covenants were more personal and less legal.
> Covenants would bind two parties together in an intimate way.
> Frequently, the consequence for violating a covenant was death.

In the Old Testament we see several covenants between men, and four covenants between God and man. When God enters a covenant, it is He who initiates the agreement.

Purpose of the Old Covenant

There were many purposes for the Mosaic covenant.

1. If the nation of Israel would obey, God would bless them so much that other nations would want to know who their God was. If the Jews would be obedient, God would bless their land and Israel would be a light to the Gentile nations. This was God's evangelism program for the nations to find Him. Other nations would look at the prosperity of the blessed Jews and want to know, "Who is your God?"

Now then, if you will indeed obey My voice and **keep My covenant**, then you shall be My own possession among all the peoples, for all the earth is Mine; and you shall be to Me a **kingdom of priests** and a **holy nation**. These are the words that you shall speak to the sons of Israel (Exod. 19:5–6).

2. That the nation of Israel would be a holy, set apart nation out of which the seed, the Messiah, would be born to save the world.

Now the promises were spoken to Abraham and to his **seed**. He does not say, "And to seeds," as referring to many, but rather to one, "And to your **seed**," that is, **Christ** (Gal. 3:16; cf. Gen. 17:7).

3. That the Jews would feel the weight of the law and call out to God for forgiveness and delivery from the curse of the law. The Laws were intended to be a schoolmaster to lead the Jews to the Messiah who would rescue them from the burden and guilt of the Law.

Therefore the Law has become our **tutor to lead us to Christ**, so that we may be justified by faith (Gal. 3:24).

4. The old covenant provided a sacrificial system for the atonement of sins. Remember, this system did not provide actual forgiveness. The blood of lambs cannot forgive sins. The Jews were never forgiven by sacrificing animals, they were forgiven "on credit" until the Lamb of God came to shed His blood for the forgiveness of their sins.

For the Law, since it has **only a shadow** of the good things to come and not the very form of things, can never, by the same sacrifices which they offer continually year by year, **make perfect** those who draw near. Otherwise, would they not have ceased to be offered, because the worshipers, having once been cleansed, would no longer have had consciousness of sins? But in those sacrifices there is a reminder of sins year by year. For it is **impossible** for the blood of bulls and goats to **take away** sins. Therefore, when He comes into the world, He says,

> "Sacrifice and offering You have **not desired**, But a **body** You have prepared for Me; In whole burnt offerings and sacrifices for sin You have taken **no pleasure**. "Then I said, 'Behold, I have come (In the scroll of the book it is written of Me) To do Your will, O God.' "

After saying above, "Sacrifices and offerings and whole burnt offerings and sacrifices for sin You have not desired, nor have You taken pleasure in them" (which are offered according to the Law), then He said, "Behold, I have come to do Your will." He **takes away** the first in order to **establish the second**. By this will we have been **sanctified** through the offering of the body of Jesus Christ **once for all** (Heb. 10:1–10).

The Centerpiece

The centerpiece of the Mosaic covenant was the tabernacle. The tabernacle was a traveling tent the Jews would schlep around the wilderness and set up every time God commanded them to camp.

Once the Jews entered the Promised Land, the tabernacle would be replaced by a permanent temple, which was very similar in design. The tabernacle and temple were integral to the Old Mosaic covenant because two major things happened there:

1. The priests would perform their daily duties, especially the blood sacrifices.
2. One day a year, on the Day of Atonement, God's special presence, His "Shekinah glory" would fall on the Holy of Holies.

A Hebrew Lesson

According to *Strong's Concordance*, the Old Testament Hebrew word for tabernacle/tent is *Mishkan*. It comes from two words:

> The prefix *mish*: the place where something happens.
> The root *shkan*: to dwell.

When you put the two words together, you have *Mishkan*: a place where God dwells. God's tabernacle was the place where God would dwell with His people when His special presence, His "shekinah glory," would descend on the tent one day a year on the Day of Atonement.

The word *Shekinah* has the letters *shkn*, just like the word *Mishkan*. God's Shekinah glory was His "special presence" glory. Note, both words have the root letters *shkn*.

Greek Lesson

As the New Testament is written in Greek, *Strong's Concordance* tells us the Greek word for tabernacle/tent is: *skaynay*. Note the similarity: the consonants in the Hebrew word for tabernacle and shekinah are *s-k-n* and the consonants in Greek for tabernacle are *s-k-n*.

Jesus Is Our Tabernacle

> And the Word became flesh, and **dwelt** among us, and we saw His glory, glory as of the only begotten from the Father, full of grace and truth (John 1:14).

The Greek word for "dwelt" is our Greek word *skaynay*. In other words, Jesus came and "tabernacled," or "pitched His tent" among us. This is a clear reference to the Old Testament tabernacle.

Just as God's shekinah glory tabernacled with His people, Jesus Christ, the second person in the trinitarian Godhead, tabernacled with us when He came to earth. The tabernacle is an Old Testament picture of Jesus. What was once a shadowy picture of God dwelling with His people became a Technicolor reality when Jesus came and tabernacled among His people.

Hebrews Makes This Clear

The theme of the New Testament Book of Hebrews is, "Jesus is better." Hebrews tells us that Jesus is better than angels. Jesus is a better covenant. Jesus is a better tabernacle. Jesus is the better everything.

God Himself was the architect for the tabernacle and it is reasonable to conclude that not only is the tent itself a type/shadow of Jesus, but so is each and every piece of furniture in the tabernacle.

Some theologians believe we should not assign a type to each object in the tabernacle, but because Hebrews 9 lists every piece of furniture in the tabernacle, it is reasonable to conclude that every item in the tabernacle is a picture of Jesus.

> Now even the first covenant had regulations of divine worship and the earthly sanctuary. For there was a **tabernacle** prepared, the outer one, in which were the **lampstand** and the **table** and the **sacred bread**; this is called the holy place. Behind the second veil there was a tabernacle which is called the Holy of Holies, having a **golden altar of incense** and the **ark of the covenant** covered on all sides with gold, in which was a golden jar holding the manna, and Aaron's rod which budded, and the tables of the covenant; and above it were the cherubim of glory overshadowing the **mercy seat** (Heb. 9:1–5).

Let's see how the tabernacle furniture was a shadowy Old Testament picture of Jesus in the New Testament.

Entrance to the Outer Courtyard

The Children of Israel entered the tabernacle through the door, which always faced east, into the outer courtyard.

Christ Is the Door

> Jesus said. . . . "I am the door; if anyone enters through Me, he will be saved" (John 10:7–9).

Laver

The laver was a water basin in which the priests washed their hands and feet daily. They could not enter the Holy Place without washing themselves in an act of ceremonial purification.

Christ Is the Laver

> Peter said to Him, "Never shall You wash my feet." Jesus answered him, "If I do not wash you, you have no part of Me" (John 13:8).

Golden Lampstand or Candlestand with Menorrah

A seven-branched candlestick made of pure gold burned olive oil night and day, serving as the only light in the tabernacle. Without this light, they

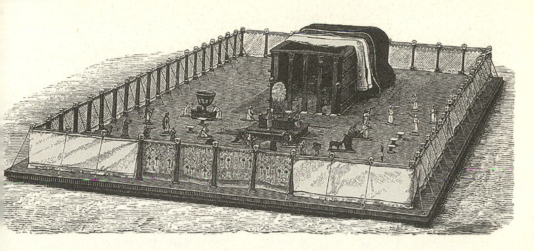

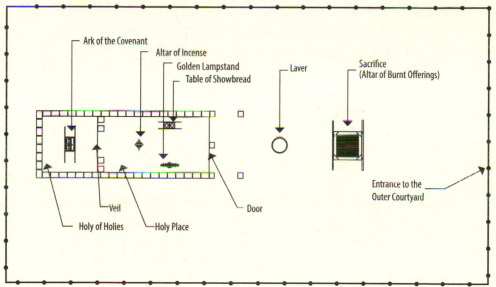

Ark of the Covenant

Altar of Incense

Golden Lampstand

Table of Showbread

Laver

Sacrifice
(Altar of Burnt Offerings)

Veil

Holy of Holies

Holy Place

Door

Entrance to the
Outer Courtyard

could not see God in His Holy Place. In darkness, the other articles would have been impossible to see.

Christ Is the Lampstand

Jesus again spoke to them, saying, "I am the Light of the world; he who follows Me will not walk in darkness, but will have the Light of life" (John 8:12).

Table of Showbread

The table with showbread was to the right as one entered the Holy Place. On it were 12 loaves of bread representing God's covenant people, Israel. The table was a place of communion and fellowship between God and people.

Christ Is the Showbread

Jesus said to them, "I am the bread of life; he who comes to Me will not hunger" (John 6:35).

Golden Altar (Altar of Incense)

The golden altar was used to burn incense. Its fragrance wafted across the mercy seat and above the other furniture. The incense burned on the altar continuously. The incense on the altar represented prayer and speaks to us on intercession. Coals to heat this altar came from the altar of sacrifice after the blood of the sacrifice dripped on them. This was God's supremely holy altar.

Christ Is the Altar of Incense

He is able also to save forever those who draw near to God through Him, since He always lives to make intercession for them (Hebrews 7:25).

Veil

The veil was a very thick curtain made of blue, purple, and scarlet fine and twined linen. No priest could enter the Holy of Holies to approach the ark of the covenant except through the veil. If a high priest passed through the veil without being sacrificially clean, God would strike him dead. God cannot have sin in His presence.

Christ Is the Veil

We have confidence to enter the holy place by the blood of Jesus, by a new and living way which He inaugurated for us through the veil, that is, His flesh (Heb. 10:19–20).

Ark of the Covenant

This special trunk-like box was the centerpiece of the Holy of Holies. On top of the ark was a lid called the mercy seat. Hovering above the mercy seat were two cherubim with outstretched wings. The ark contained the two tablets of the Ten Commandments, a pot of manna, and Aaron's rod that budded.

One time a year, on the Day of Atonement, the blood of a goat was placed on the mercy seat to cover the sins of the people. It was there above the mercy seat that God hovered in the pillar of cloud and offered propitiation for the people.

Christ Is the Mercy Seat

Jesus Christ, whom God displayed publicly as a propitiation in His blood through faith (Romans 3:24–25).

Priests

The priests were the mediators between God and man. The high priest was the head priest.

Christ Is the High Priest

For it was fitting for us to have such a high priest, holy, innocent, undefiled, separated from sinners and exalted above the heavens (Hebrews 7:26).

Sacrifice

Yearly, an unblemished lamb was slaughtered for the covering of sins of the individual. The priests would place their hands on the lamb, symbolically transferring the sins of the people to the lamb that would be slaughtered for the covering, but not the forgiveness, of sins.

Christ Is the Sacrifice

By this will we have been sanctified through the offering of the body of Jesus Christ once for all (Hebrews 10:10).

Something Is Missing

Did you notice a piece of furniture is strangely absent? Hint: day after day, year after year, the priests entered in and out of the tabernacle to offer sacrifices. They stood on their feet hour after hour and never sat down because their work was never done.

The piece of furniture that was missing in the tabernacle was a chair. The old covenant priests continually offered sacrifices as a picture of the greater sacrifice that was needed. They never rested from their labor (Heb. 10:11).

Jesus Christ Sat Down

Jesus Christ finished His sacrificial work to forgive sins once and for all time (Heb. 9:15–28; Matt. 26:28), rose from the dead (Luke 24:6; 1 Cor. 15:4, 12–17) and ascended into heaven (John 24:5; Acts 1:9).

Paul Washer vividly describes what happens next by applying Psalm 24:7–10.[1]

> Jesus, the Great High Priest, triumphantly approached the gates of heaven and demanded, "Lift up your heads, O gates, and be lifted up, O ancient doors, that the King of glory may come in!"
>
> From inside there was a reply, "Who is the King of glory?"
>
> Jesus thundered, "The LORD strong and mighty, the LORD mighty in battle. Lift up your heads, O gates, and lift them up, O ancient doors, that the King of glory may come in!"
>
> Again, the attendants asked, "Who is this King of glory?"
>
> Jesus shattered the heavens, "The LORD of hosts, He is the King of glory."
>
> As the gates swung open, for the first time ever, a human entered heaven.
>
> Jesus Christ, the resurrected God-man marched through the gates toward His throne at the right hand of God. And He sat down (Heb. 10:12).

The sacrificial work of our Great High Priest was so total, so perfect, so complete, He triumphantly rested from His labor.

> Every priest **stands daily** ministering and offering time after time the same sacrifices, which can **never take away sins**; but He, having offered **one sacrifice** for sins **for all time**, **sat down** at the right hand of God, waiting from that time onward until His enemies be made a footstool for His feet. For by one offering He has **perfected for all time** those who are sanctified (Heb. 10:11–14).

Where Does God Tabernacle Now?

God the Son, Jesus Christ, is now seated in authority at the right hand of God the Father (Matt. 26:64; Heb. 1:3; Ps. 110:1). That does not mean He has abandoned us.

---

1. https://www.youtube.com/watch?v=a11ASw5NRUw#t=224

While Jesus was preparing the disciples for His death, He told them, "But I tell you the truth, it is to your advantage that I go away; for if I do not go away, the Helper will not come to you; but if I go, I will send Him to you" (John 16:7).

Jesus promised to send the Helper, His Holy Spirit, the third person in the trinitarian Godhead, to those who would repent and believe in Him to the glory of God the Father. Jesus is now in heaven, but His Holy Spirit dwells in those who believe.

> Blessed be the God and Father of our Lord Jesus Christ, who has blessed us with every spiritual blessing in the heavenly places **in Christ**, just as He chose us in Him **before the foundation of the world**, that we would be holy and blameless before Him.
>
> **In love** He predestined us to adoption as sons through Jesus Christ to Himself, according to the kind intention of His will, **to the praise of the glory of His grace**, which He freely bestowed on us in the Beloved.
>
> **In Him** we have redemption through His blood, the forgiveness of our trespasses, according to the riches of His grace which He lavished on us. In all wisdom and insight He made known to us the mystery of His will, according to His **kind intention** which He purposed in Him with a view to an administration suitable to the fullness of the times, that is, the summing up of all things in Christ, things in the heavens and things on the earth.
>
> **In Him** also we have obtained an inheritance, having been **predestined** according to His purpose who works all things after the counsel of His will, to the end that we who were the first to hope in Christ would be to the praise of His glory.
>
> **In Him**, you also, after listening to the message of truth, the gospel of your salvation — having also believed, you were **sealed in Him with the Holy Spirit** of promise, who is given as a pledge of our inheritance, with a view to the redemption of God's own possession, **to the praise of His glory** (Eph. 1:3–14).

Because God's Holy Spirit tabernacles in His people, the Apostle Paul wrote, "Do you not know that your body is a **temple of the Holy Spirit** who is in you, whom you have from God, and that you are not your own? (1 Cor. 6:19).

And again Paul said:

But if the Spirit of Him who raised Jesus from the dead **dwells in you**, He who raised Christ Jesus from the dead will also give life to your mortal bodies through **His Spirit who dwells in you** (Rom. 8:11).

If You Are a Christian

Each individual Christian is a living temple. In the Old Testament, God's presence descended on the tabernacle one day a year; because of the work of Jesus, God dwells perpetually in the heart of every believer. God actually tabernacles in you. You are a temple of the Holy Spirit.

The Holy Spirit of God is at work in you, granting you the power to be conformed more and more into the image of Jesus Christ so you can glorify God the Father and one day join Him in His heavenly tabernacle.

If You Are Not a Christian

God is not dwelling in you. God is not your friend, He is your enemy.

For the mind set on the flesh is death, but the mind set on the Spirit is life and peace, because the mind set on the flesh is hostile toward God; for it does not subject itself to the law of God, for it is not even able to do so, and those who are in the flesh cannot please God (Rom. 8:6–8).

The world tells us we are "all children of God." In one sense, that is correct as God is the One who gives life to every living thing. But because of the Fall, our minds are actually at enmity with God. That is why we need Jesus. That is why He came to this earth, to restore us to a right relationship with God.

And although you were formerly alienated and hostile in mind, engaged in evil deeds, yet He has now reconciled you in His fleshly body through death, in order to present you before Him holy and blameless and beyond reproach (Col. 1:21–22).

For if while we were enemies we were reconciled to God through the death of His Son, much more, having been reconciled, we shall be saved by His life. And not only this, but we also exult in God through our Lord Jesus Christ, through whom we have now received the reconciliation (Rom. 5:10–11).

That is what makes grace so amazing. God does not just save sinless people. God saves wretches. God saves His enemies.

If you are in Christ, God is no longer your enemy. But if you are not, you are under the control of the devil.

> The one who practices sin is of the devil; for the devil has sinned from the beginning. The Son of God appeared for this purpose, to destroy the works of the devil (1 John 3:8, cf. also: John 8:44; Matt. 13:38).

If you have rejected God's marvelous offer of amazing grace, these words from Hebrews are for you.

> How much **severer** punishment do you think he will deserve who has trampled under foot the Son of God, and has regarded as unclean the **blood of the covenant** by which he was sanctified, and has insulted the Spirit of grace? For we know Him who said, "**Vengeance** is Mine, I will repay." And again, "The Lord will judge His people." It is a **terrifying** thing to fall into the hands of the living God (Heb. 10:29–31).

Why would you want that? Why would you want to continue living as an enemy of God when you could have God living in you?

You do not need to fall into the hands of the living God. You do not need to be on the receiving end of His wrath. You do not need to go to hell. Instead of being punished by God and separated from Him forever, He will deign to dwell in you now so you can live with Him for eternity.

A sinful man cannot endure the presence of the Holy God. Jesus Christ tented among His people so that you could be cleansed and brought into the presence of your Maker. Why would you want to dwell in hell when you could tabernacle with the God who loves you and died to save you?

Repent and put your trust in the perfect sacrifice, Jesus Christ and be reconciled to God.

Only God could write a story like this through dozens of authors over thousands of years with one theme.

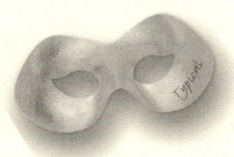

Typical

Chapter 12

Read This!

This is the best chapter of the book. Why? God Himself inspired these words to be written just for you.

Now that you have the backdrop for covenants, sacrifices, and the tabernacle in the Old Testament, take the time to read these three chapters from the New Testament Book of Hebrews.

Witness the amazing cohesiveness of the Bible. Moses wrote about the old covenant and the tabernacle in the 15th century B.C. Hebrews was written in the 1st century A.D. It is impossible to imagine that these words are not inspired by God Himself. Man could not concoct such a brilliant scheme.

This translation is the New Living Translation.

Hebrews 8

Here is the main point: We have a High Priest who **sat down** in the place of honor beside the throne of the majestic God in heaven.

There he ministers in the heavenly **Tabernacle**, the true place of worship that was built by the Lord and not by human hands.

And since every high priest is required to offer gifts and **sacrifices**, our **High Priest** must make an offering, too. If he were here on earth, he would not even be a priest, since there already are priests who offer the gifts required by the law. They serve in a system of worship that is only a **copy**, a **shadow** of the real one in heaven. For when Moses was getting ready to build the Tabernacle, God gave him this warning: "Be sure that you make everything according to the pattern I have shown you here on the mountain."

But now Jesus, our High Priest, has been given a ministry that is **far superior** to the old priesthood, for he is the one who **mediates** for us a far **better covenant** with God, based on better promises.

If the first covenant had been faultless, there would have been no need for a second covenant to replace it. But when God found fault with the people, he said:

> "The day is coming, says the LORD,
> > when I will make a **new covenant**
> > with the people of Israel and Judah.
> This covenant will not be like the one
> > I made with their ancestors
> when I took them by the hand
> > and led them out of the land of Egypt.
> They **did not remain faithful** to my covenant,
> > so I turned my back on them, says the LORD.
> But this is the **new covenant** I will make
> > with the people of Israel on that day, says the LORD:
> I will put my laws in their minds,
> > and I will write them on their hearts.
> I will be their God
> > and they will be my people.
> And they will not need to teach their neighbors,
> > nor will they need to teach their relatives,
> > saying, 'You should know the LORD.'
> For everyone, from the least to the greatest,
> > will know me already.
> And I will **forgive their wickedness**,
> > and I will **never again remember their sins**."

When God speaks of a **"new"** covenant, it means He has made the first one **obsolete**. It is now out of date and will soon disappear.

Hebrews 9

That **first covenant** between God and Israel had regulations for worship and a place of worship here on earth. There were two rooms in that **Tabernacle**. In the first room were **a lamp stand, a table, and sacred loaves of bread on the table**. This room was called the Holy Place. Then there was a **curtain**, and behind the curtain was the second room called the Most Holy Place. In that room were a **gold incense altar** and a wooden chest called the **Ark of the Covenant**, which was covered with gold on all sides. . . .

When these things were all in place, the priests regularly entered the first room as they performed their religious duties. But only the high priest ever entered the Most Holy Place, and only once a year. And he **always** offered blood for his own sins and for the sins the people had committed in ignorance. By these regulations the Holy Spirit revealed that the entrance to the Most Holy Place was not freely open as long as the Tabernacle and the system it represented were still in use.

This is an **illustration pointing to the present time**. For the gifts and sacrifices that the priests offer are **not able** to cleanse the consciences of the people who bring them. For that old system deals only with food and drink and various cleansing ceremonies — physical regulations that were in effect only until a **better system** could be established.

Christ Is the Perfect Sacrifice

So Christ has now become the High Priest over all the good things that have come. He has entered that greater, **more perfect Tabernacle in heaven**, which was not made by human hands and is not part of this created world. With his own blood — not the blood of goats and calves — he entered the Most Holy Place **once for all time** and **secured** our redemption forever.

Under the old system, the blood of goats and bulls and the ashes of a young cow could cleanse people's bodies from ceremonial impurity. Just think how **much more** the blood of Christ will purify **our consciences** from sinful deeds so that we can worship the living

God. For by the power of the eternal Spirit, Christ offered himself to God as a **perfect sacrifice** for our sins. That is why he is the one who mediates a **new covenant** between God and people, so that all who are called can receive the eternal inheritance God has promised them. For Christ died to **set them free** from the penalty of the sins they had committed under that first covenant.

Now when someone leaves a will, it is necessary to prove that the person who made it is dead. The will goes into effect only after the person's death. While the person who made it is still alive, the will cannot be put into effect.

That is why even the first covenant was put into effect with the **blood** of an animal. For after Moses had read each of God's commandments to all the people, he took the **blood** of calves and goats, along with water, and sprinkled both the book of God's law and all the people, using hyssop branches and scarlet wool. Then he said, "This **blood** confirms the covenant God has made with you." And in the same way, he sprinkled blood on the Tabernacle and on everything used for worship. In fact, according to the law of Moses, nearly everything was purified with **blood**. For **without the shedding of blood, there is no forgiveness**.

That is why the Tabernacle and everything in it, which were **copies** of things in heaven, had to be purified by the blood of animals. But the real things in heaven had to be purified with **far better sacrifices** than the blood of animals.

For Christ did not enter into a holy place made with human hands, which was **only a copy** of the true one in heaven. He entered into heaven itself to appear now before God on our behalf. And he did not enter heaven to offer himself again and again, like the high priest here on earth who enters the Most Holy Place year after year with the blood of an animal. If that had been necessary, Christ would have had to die again and again, ever since the world began. But now, **once for all time**, he has appeared at the end of the age to remove sin by his own death as a sacrifice.

And just as each person is destined to die once and after that comes judgment, so also Christ died **once for all time** as a sacrifice to **take away** the sins of many people. He will come again, not to deal with our sins, but to bring salvation to all who are eagerly waiting for him.

Hebrews 10

The old system under the law of Moses was **only a shadow**, a dim **preview** of the good things to come, not the good things themselves. The sacrifices under that system were repeated **again and again**, year after year, but they were never able to provide perfect cleansing for those who came to worship. If they could have provided perfect cleansing, the sacrifices would have stopped, for the worshipers would have been purified once for all time, and their feelings of guilt would have disappeared.

But instead, those sacrifices actually reminded them of their sins year after year. For it is **not possible** for the blood of bulls and goats to take away sins. That is why, when Christ came into the world, he said to God,

> "You did not want animal sacrifices or sin offerings.
> But you have given me a body to offer.
> You were not pleased with burnt offerings
> or other offerings for sin.
> Then I said, 'Look, I have come to do your will, O God —
> as is **written about me** in the Scriptures.' "

First, Christ said, "You did not want animal sacrifices or sin offerings or burnt offerings or other offerings for sin, nor were you pleased with them" (though they are required by the law of Moses). Then he said, "Look, I have come to do your will." He **cancels the first covenant** in order to put the second into effect. For God's will was for us to be made holy by the sacrifice of the body of Jesus Christ, **once for all time**.

Under the old covenant, the priest stands and ministers before the altar day after day, offering the same sacrifices again and again, which **can never take away sins**. But our High Priest offered himself to God as a **single sacrifice** for sins, **good for all time**. Then he **sat down** in the place of honor at God's right hand. There he waits until his enemies are humbled and made a footstool under his feet. For by that **one offering** he forever **made perfect** those who are being made holy.

And the Holy Spirit also testifies that this is so. For he says,

> "This is the **new covenant** I will make
> with my people on that day, says the LORD:

> I will put my laws in their hearts,
> and I will write them on their minds."

Then he says,

> "I will never again remember
> their sins and lawless deeds."

And when sins have been forgiven, there is no need to offer any more sacrifices.

A Call to Persevere

And so, dear brothers and sisters, we can boldly enter heaven's Most Holy Place because of the blood of Jesus. By his death, Jesus opened a new and life-giving way **through the curtain** into the Most Holy Place. And since we have a great High Priest who rules over God's house, let us go right into the **presence of God** with sincere hearts fully trusting him. For our guilty consciences have been sprinkled with Christ's blood to make us **clean**, and our bodies have been washed with pure water. . . .

Dear friends, if we deliberately continue sinning after we have received knowledge of the truth, there is no longer any sacrifice that will cover these sins. There is only the **terrible expectation** of God's judgment and the **raging fire** that will consume his enemies. For anyone who refused to obey the law of Moses was put to death without mercy on the testimony of two or three witnesses. Just think **how much worse** the punishment will be for those who have trampled on the Son of God, and have treated the **blood of the covenant**, which made us holy, as if it were common and unholy, and have insulted and disdained the Holy Spirit who brings God's mercy to us. For we know the one who said,

> "I will take revenge.
> I will pay them back."

He also said,

> "The LORD will judge his own people."

It is a **terrible thing** to fall into the hands of the living God. . . .

So do not throw away this confident trust in the Lord. Remember the great reward it brings you! Patient endurance is what you need now, so that you will continue to do God's will. Then you will receive all that he has promised.

> "For in just a little while,
> the **Coming One** will come and not delay.
> And my righteous ones will live by faith.
> But I will take **no pleasure** in anyone who turns away."

But we are not like those who turn away from God to their own destruction. We are the faithful ones, whose **souls will be saved**.

Only God could write a story like this through dozens of authors over thousands of years with one theme: Jesus Christ, the tabernacle.

Year	Event

250

A.D. 33: Jesus crucified
A.D. 30: Jesus begins ministry
A.D. 26: John the Baptist begins preaching

0   0: Jesus is born

397–5 B.C.: The silent years

250

397 B.C.: Malachi is Israel's last prophet until John the Baptist

500   515 B.C.: Jerusalem rebuilt and temple completed
536 B.C.: Jews start returning to Jerusalem
586 B.C.: Southern Kingdom falls to Babylon

750   721 B.C.: Northern Kingdom falls to Assyria

975 B.C.: Israel split in two

1000   1004 B.C.: Solomon's temple completed
1015 B.C.: Solomon becomes king
1055 B.C.: David becomes king

1250

1451 B.C.: The Jews enter the Promised Land
1491–1451 B.C.: The Jews wander the desert
1500   1491 B.C.: Moses leads the Exodus out of Egypt

1700–1574 B.C.: Joseph and his brothers have lots of babies
1750   1739 B.C.: Joseph sold into slavery in Egypt

1836 B.C.: Jacob born

1896 B.C.: Isaac born

2000   1996 B.C. Abraham born

2250

2349 B.C.: Noah and the Global Flood

2500

2750

3000

3250

Timeline

4004 B.C. — A.D. 33

3500

3750

4000   4004 B.C.: Creation, Adam and Eve, Cain and Abel

A SON OF GOD

Chapter 13

Jesus Is the Sabbath

Here's an offer you shouldn't refuse. Jesus Christ commanded, "Come to Me, all who are weary and heavy-laden and I will give you rest" (Matt. 11:28).

That should make you go, "Ahhh." Because whether you know it or not, you are working. Hard.

Work Righteousness Is Our Natural Bent

Every person on the planet has a little courtroom in their brain called "the conscience." Your conscience is that voice in your noggin that nags you when you have done something wrong, and everyone has one. Everyone.

This alone should cause the atheist to backslide and become agnostic. Evolution simply can't explain why every culture shares the same basic set of values: no stealing, no murder, no Lady Gaga. Wait, sorry, a Lady Gaga-free society should be the law.

Skeptics point to a few cannibals here or there, but even cannibals don't like being cannibals. Go ahead, ask one. If you can.

Overall, morality in every culture is the same: lying, cheating, hurting, dishonoring parents are verboten worldwide. Why?

> For when Gentiles who do not have the Law do instinctively the things of the Law, these, not having the Law, are a law to themselves, in that they show the work of the **Law written in their hearts**, their **conscience** bearing witness and their thoughts alternately **accusing** or else **defending** them, on the day when, according to my gospel, God will judge the secrets of men through Christ Jesus (Rom. 2:14–16).

Where did the conscience come from? Certainly not from Charles Darwin. God created and implemented the concept.

An Atheist Conundrum

If you are an atheist, you have an impossible time explaining why you know that murder is wrong. Without an objective standard for morality, you can only have preferences.

The only way to know you are speeding is if the law has determined a particular speed and posted the number. If no authority determined how fast we can or cannot drive, then there would only be speed preferences and nobody could give you a ticket for driving 70 in a school zone.

Without an objective lawgiver, there are no laws, only preferences.

God Is the Reason for Math

If you hate algebra and trigonometry, whatever that is, please don't let this make you bitter. Math exists because God exists.

If the world is randomly designed through time and chance, then math should never be consistent. Math exists because a Creator exists who designed the universe with laws and intelligence. What makes two plus two always four? God.

Math is consistent because God is consistent.

God Is the Reason for Science

Every time a scientist, whether Christian or not, does an experiment anticipating a consistent outcome, he is giving a hat tip to God. Without God, there would be no scientific laws. Without God, experiments would never have the same outcome twice.

The field of science was championed by Christians who realized this and decided to figure out exactly how God created and sustains the world. They attempted to "think God's thoughts after Him."[1]

Every atheist who believes in morality, gravity, and does math is a closeted believer.

The Creator Is the Reason for Creation

If Richard Dawkins wants to prove that God doesn't exist, then he needs to make all the stuff go away. Short of that, it is evident there is a Creator. Why? Because there is a creation.

> The heavens are **telling** of the glory of God;
> And their expanse is **declaring** the work of His hands.
> Day to day pours forth **speech**,
> And night to night **reveals** knowledge.
> There is no speech, nor are there words;
> Their voice is not heard (Ps. 19:1–3).

There really is no reason to prove that God exists — it is self-evident. Even a child intuits that God exists. Nobody will be able to stand on judgment day and ask, "Why didn't you tell me?"

What about the Natives on Boingo Boingo?

What happens to natives on Boingo Boingo who never hear about Jesus Christ — does God send them to hell?

1. The Boingo Boinguese have heard a sermon from God each and every day of their lives. It is the sermon entitled: Creation. The creation is perpetually screaming to anyone who will listen, "Look! God exists."
2. The Boingo Boinguese have a conscience that should cause them to cry out to the Creator, "Help me. Rescue me."
3. This may sound a little harsh, but the question is not, "Should someone go to hell?" The question should be, "Has that person sinned?" The painful truth is that everyone sins and God is not obliged to save everyone. It is only by His grace that He saves anyone. Everyone deserves to go to hell and God is not beholden to save anyone.

---

1. A phrase first used by Johann Kepler (1571–1630).

4. Everyone knows that God exists. They don't know Him in a saving way, but everyone knows God.

Everyone Knows Who God Is

> For the wrath of God is revealed from heaven against all ungodliness and unrighteousness of men who **suppress the truth in unrighteousness**, because **that which is known about God is evident within them**; for God **made it evident** to them. For since the creation of the world His invisible attributes, His eternal power and divine nature, **have been clearly seen**, being understood through what has been made, so that they are **without excuse**. For even though **they knew God**, they did not honor Him as God or give thanks, but they became futile in their speculations, and their foolish heart was darkened (Rom. 1:18–21).

To be clear, everyone is not in a right relationship with God, but they do know who He is. Therefore, everyone is without excuse for not responding to the inner light that God has graciously provided them.

Two Responses

Humans have two responses to the conscience and innate knowledge that God exists:

1. They suppress the truth so they can live unrighteously (Rom. 1:18).
2. They suppress the truth and create their own god which allows them to work hard to appease their man-made deities' demands.

Perhaps you have fashioned a god in your mind that can be appeased by your good deeds. Perhaps you think that your god is satisfied with an occasional act of kindness or visit to a church. You are not the only one.

Every Other Religious System Is Works-Based

Because of the conscience, man has concocted all kinds of religious schemes in an attempt to feel guilt-free. Notice the consistent theme in each and every world religion except biblical Christianity.

> Roman Catholicism: grace plus good deeds, plus sacraments, plus last rites, plus confession, plus penance.

> Mormonism: works plus grace.
> Jehovah's Witnesses: grace plus good works.
> Hinduism: The only way to be liberated is through social and religious obligations: in other words, works.
> Buddhism: Ceaseless labor in an effort to throw off karma and attain extinction (nirvana). That is both work righteousness and depressing.
> Islam: Each follower must perform the five pillars of Islam (Shahada, declaring that there is no other god but Allah and Muhammad is his prophet; Salat, five prayers daily; Zakat, give 2.5 percent of income to the poor; Sawm, fast during the month of Ramadan; Hajj, take at least one trip to Mecca during one's lifetime). That is a lot of work.

It is Jesus Christ and Jesus Christ alone who announces, "My yoke is easy and My burden is light" (Matt. 11:30). In other words, salvation is by grace alone, through faith alone, in Jesus Christ alone. No works. No lists. No do's. It has all been done for you by Jesus. Why?

1. All of your righteous deeds are like filthy rags (Isa. 64:6). We don't even have the ability to do good works that appease God. All of our good deeds are contaminated.
2. Justice does not work on a balance system. Imagine a guilty criminal telling the judge, "Your honor, I know I robbed that bank, but I gave some of the money to the poor." The judge would laugh. Good works do not offset crimes.
3. God will not be bribed. Imagine a criminal telling a judge, "Your honor, I know I am guilty, but I baked these cookies for you." The judge would accuse the criminal of trying to bribe him. God will not be bought.
4. If you could do good deeds to contribute to your salvation, then you would deserve some credit for going to heaven. God insists on getting all of the credit because He is the One who has done everything to earn forgiveness for you (Eph. 2:8–9).

What about Judaism?

Even though Judaism was never intended to be a work righteous religion, it had become works-based by the time Jesus came to earth. Biblical salvation was always intended to be "by grace alone."

What then shall we say that Abraham, our forefather according to the flesh, has found? For if Abraham was justified by works, he has something to **boast** about, but not before God. For what does the Scripture say? "Abraham **believed** God, and it was **credited to him as righteousness**."

Now to the one who **works**, his wage is not credited as a favor, but as what is due. But to the one who does not work, but **believes** in Him who justifies the ungodly, his **faith** is **credited as righteousness**, just as David also speaks of the blessing on the man to whom God **credits righteousness** apart from works.

"Blessed are those whose lawless deeds have been **forgiven**, And whose sins have been covered. "Blessed is the man whose sin the Lord will not take into account" (Rom. 4:1–8).

Unfortunately, most of the Jews missed grace. Instead of responding to the Law by calling out to God for help, they responded in typical human form, "We'll do it. We will keep the laws and God will be pleased with us."

That is why the Jewish leaders created a manual for keeping the Ten Commandments. Instead of receiving the Ten Commandments and crying out to God for the Messiah to deliver them, they created a rulebook that makes Obamacare legislation look like bedtime reading.

Sabbath Laws

The fourth commandment given to Moses and the children of Israel in the wilderness was, "Remember the Sabbath day, to keep it holy" (Exod. 20:8). But the Bible doesn't give instructions on HOW to keep the last day of the week holy. So what did the Jewish religious leaders do? They created 39 categories of laws with hundreds of do's and don'ts.

Here are just some of the 613 Sabbath rules invented by the Jewish rabbis recorded in the Mishna. No, these are not made up.

> No grey hair plucking. That was work.
> No chair moving as you could make a furrow in the dirt and that is tantamount to farming.
> No bathing because you could spill water and you would be working when you wiped it up.
> No mule or horseback riding; not because that was work, but you might be tempted to break a switch to whip the horse. That is work.

> No knot tying.
> No writing; at least no more than two letters.
> No fire extinguishing, even if great damage could result from the fire.

On and on and on they go. Sabbath rules became the centerpiece of Jewish religious life as a system for earning forgiveness. Talk about a burden.

How to Get to Heaven

The rabbis had turned the Sabbath gift of rest into a method for working one's way to heaven. What made a Jew a faithful Jew was obedience to the rabbinical Sabbath rules. It is safe to say that this was their pet commandment.

The Pharisees were the Sabbath rule writers. They were the Sabbath rule keepers. They were the Sabbath rule enforcers. Don't mess with their Sabbath.

WWF Smackdown

The scene you are about to witness is a veritable cage match.

The Jewish leaders had turned God's system of grace into such a burden that the Jews must have dreaded their day off. Immediately after Jesus announced that His "burden was easy and His yoke light," Matthew shares this encounter, and it is a serious smackdown.

In one corner, the self-righteous religious experts. In the other corner, Jesus.

> At that time Jesus went through the grainfields on the **Sabbath**, and His disciples became hungry and began to **pick the heads** *of grain* and eat. But when the Pharisees saw *this*, they said to Him, "Look, Your disciples do what is **not lawful** to do on a Sabbath."
>
> But He said to them, "**Have you not read** what David did when he became hungry, he and his companions, how he entered the house of God, and they ate the consecrated bread, which was **not lawful** for him to eat nor for those with him, but for the priests alone? Or **have you not read** in the Law, that on the **Sabbath** the priests in the temple break the **Sabbath** and are innocent?
>
> "But I say to you that **something greater** than the temple is here. But **if you had known** what this means, 'I desire compassion, and not a sacrifice,' you would not have condemned the innocent.
>
> "For the Son of Man is **Lord of the Sabbath**" (Matt. 12:1–8).

Kaboom! That was a pile driver. Jesus didn't just cross a line, He sprinted over it and then pointed back at the Pharisees, the teachers of the Law, and said, "You don't know your Bibles!"

1. Jesus had not broken a biblical Law, but a man-made religious rule.
2. The Bible actually approved of gleaning wheat when you were hungry (Deut. 23:25).
3. Jesus used King David as an example of eating the temple bread when he was starving to teach that the Sabbath was not supposed to be a yoke, but a blessing.
4. This is the biggie; Jesus proclaimed that He is the "Lord of the Sabbath." Kerpow!

Do You Remember That Verse?

Perhaps the foundational verse in the Bible that teaches Old Testament people, places, and things can be types and shadows of Jesus is Colossians 2:16–17.

> Therefore no one is to act as your judge in regard to food or drink or in respect to a **festival** or a new moon or a **Sabbath** day — things which are a mere **shadow** of what is to come; but the **substance** belongs to **Christ**.

When Jesus told the Pharisees that He is the "Lord of the Sabbath," He was basically saying, "The Old Testament Sabbath is a picture of ME! Don't you read the Scriptures?"

How much of a smack to the kisser was that? They responded by plotting to kill Him. They were not just mad, they were insulted, humiliated, and infuriated. The so-called "Teachers of the Law" revealed they didn't understand the Law at all.

What Is the Sabbath?

Most people probably think "Remember the Sabbath to keep it holy," is the least important of the Big Ten. It is not.

If you throw a plate at your wife during an argument, you are in big trouble. But if you take off your wedding ring and whip it at her, you are in the doghouse. Why? Because your wedding ring is a symbol of your covenant to "love and cherish her 'til death do you part."

To throw your wedding ring at your spouse is to spurn your covenant.

The Old Testament Sabbath is like your wedding ring; it is a symbol of the Mosaic covenant between God and His people. To break the Sabbath was to defile the thing it represents, Israel's covenant relationship with God.

To break the Sabbath was like burning the flag. To break the Sabbath was to spurn God and all He had done for Israel. To break the Sabbath was akin to asking God for a divorce. That is why the death sentence was prescribed for violating the Sabbath (Exod. 31:12–17).

When Was the Sabbath Initiated?

The Sabbath did not start at Sinai when Moses received the Ten Commandments. The Sabbath was initiated at creation.

> **Days 1–5:** God made all the stuff: the earth, planets, water, trees, vegetation.
> **Days 5–6:** God made all the animals without a spirit: fish, fowl, animals, reptiles.
> **Day 6:** The last thing God made was human beings in His image with an eternal soul.

As the week progressed, the value of the things created increased from inanimate to animate; from without a soul to soul-bearing human beings. A plant has more value than a rock. A dog has more value than a plant, and a human has more value than every created thing. Share that with a PETA member and watch their head explode.

> **Day 7:** God rests.

Wait a second, if the creation week advanced in importance, the formula seems to collapse on day 7. How could "God rests" on day 7 be better than His creation of little ol' us on day 6? For the very same reason: the creation week was advancing in order of importance.

As special as humans are (and we are), the culmination of the creation week was not the creation of man, but God resting and enjoying Himself and His work. On the seventh day, God rested and exulted in the glory of His labors. The entire creation week was moving toward a goal of rest, contemplation, and enjoyment of God.

Exodus 20

Two millennia after creation, the Jews were wandering around the desert like the husband of a Black Friday shopper at the mega-mall when God gave Moses the Ten Commandments. Here is commandment number four:

> Remember the **sabbath day**, to keep it holy. Six days you shall **labor** and do all your **work**, but the seventh day is a sabbath of the Lord your God; in it you shall **not do any work**, you or your son or your daughter, your male or your female servant or your cattle or your sojourner who stays with you. For in six days **the Lord made** the heavens and the earth, the sea and all that is in them, and **rested** on the seventh day; **therefore** the Lord blessed the sabbath day and made it holy (Exod. 20:8–11).

In their corporate lives, the Jews were to work for six days then rest and enjoy God for one day, just like God did at creation. For six days, the Jews did back-breaking labor and rested for one day and focused on God. Then back to work.

Rinse and repeat.

Rinse and repeat.

Rinse and repeat.

This cycle was relentless. Work, rest. Work, rest. Work, rest. In a very tangible way, the Jews were reminded every week that a permanent rest is coming.

Jesus Is the Lord of the Sabbath

Enter Jesus, who announced that the Sabbath was merely a shadowy picture of Himself; He is the Lord of the Sabbath. He invited the Jews to rest from their work righteous efforts to earn God's favor and REST IN HIM. When a person rests in Jesus and His accomplishments, every second of every day is a Sabbath rest.

> So there remains **a Sabbath rest for the people of God**. For the one who has **entered His rest** has himself also **rested from his works**, as God did from His (Heb. 4:9–10).

Every religious system in the world besides Christianity demands, "Work." Jesus invites you to rest. The God whom you have offended kept every law you have broken and now He bids you to stop trying to work your way to heaven and rest in Him. Have you ever had a better offer?

Other world religions demand, "Do!" Jesus proclaims, "Done."

What About the Ten Commandments?

Perhaps you are wondering about the Ten Commandments. If we don't have to "keep the Sabbath," isn't that a violation of one of the Big Ten? Great question.

The Book of Hebrews makes it clear, the old covenant is gone. Kaput. Blotto. Finished.

> For **if** that **first** covenant had been faultless, there would have been no occasion sought for a **second**. For finding fault with them, He says,
> "Behold, days are coming, says the Lord,
> When I will effect a **new covenant**
> With the house of Israel and with the house of Judah;
> Not like the covenant which I made with their fathers
> On the day when I took them by the hand
> To lead them out of the land of Egypt;
> For **they did not** continue in My covenant,
> And I did not care for them," says the Lord. . . .
> "For I will be merciful to their iniquities,
> And I will remember their sins **no more**."
> When He said, "A new covenant," He has **made the first obsolete**. But whatever is becoming obsolete and growing old is ready to disappear (Heb. 8:7–13).

The old covenant is no longer in affect. We have a new and better covenant purchased and mediated by Jesus Christ. That does not mean we forget the lessons, principles, and theology of the old covenant, but it is no longer in effect. It has no power over us.

So what do we do with the Ten Commandments? We keep nine out of ten of them. Why? Because nine of the Ten Commandments are reiterated in the New Testament. The only commandment that does not reappear in the new covenant is . . . you guessed it, the fourth commandment to keep the Sabbath holy.

What About Church?

Perhaps you are wondering about church. If we don't have to "keep the Sabbath," then why do we go to church on Sunday? Another great question.

We go to church because we are commanded to not forsake "our own assembling together" (Heb. 10:25). We choose to gather on Sunday, the day

Jesus rose from the dead, because that is the day the early Church gathered and we have maintained that pattern to this day (Acts 20:7; 1 Cor. 16:2).

We don't go to church on Saturday because that was merely a picture of the greater rest that Jesus secured when He rose from the dead on Easter Sunday.

Ultimately, as long as you assemble to hear the Word, celebrate the Lord's Supper and baptisms, pray, worship, and practice church discipline if necessary, it does not matter what day you gather because every day is a day of rest for the Christian.

How Light Is Jesus' Yoke?

Jesus' yoke is so light that most people hate Him for it.

Our natural, self-righteous propensity is to think we can earn God's favor by doing good deeds, just like the Pharisees. Jesus smashes that notion when He says, "I will give YOU rest" (Matt. 11:28; emphasis added). You can't do it. Your best efforts are so rotten they only contribute to your condemnation. Your best days are not even close to being good enough.

Jesus Christ is a "stumbling block" (1 Cor.1:23) and "a stone of stumbling and a rock of offense" (1 Pet.2:8), because He crushes our self-righteous pride by declaring us entirely unable to contribute anything to our redemption. Most hate that and hate Him because of it. We like to work for our salvation.

All roads that claim to lead to God are an uphill climb. Jesus has paved the way for you to be totally and completely forgiven. It is hard to imagine that He would go through unimaginable effort to purchase your forgiveness yet permit you to pick a work-righteous system to climb your way into His presence.

"God Resists the Proud"

Are you still trying to somehow please God through your "good deeds"? Is Jesus still a stumbling block to you because you hate the idea of having to receive total mercy?

Is your opinion of yourself so high? Do you not see how misplaced your trust in yourself is? Will you cling to your pride and your works when Jesus offers you complete and total rest?

Hear Him appeal to you now:

"God is opposed to the proud, but gives grace to the humble."
Submit therefore to God. Resist the devil and he will flee from you.

Draw near to God and He will draw near to you. **Cleanse** your hands, **you sinners**; and purify your hearts, you double-minded. Be miserable and **mourn** and weep [for yourself and for your sins]; let your laughter be turned into mourning and your joy to gloom. **Humble yourselves** in the presence of the Lord, and He will exalt you (James 4:6–10).

Are you tired of striving? Are you exhausted from working? Are you weary and heavy laden with guilt?

Lose your pride. Lay down your good works. Run to Jesus, the Lord of the Sabbath. He will give you rest.

Chapter 14

Jesus Is Seven Festivals

God is not a crabby curmudgeon. The true God is a God of joy who invites — no, He commands — His people to celebrate.

While the Jews were mundanely wandering the wilderness, God ordered them to celebrate His goodness seven times a year. These festivals were not meant to be a humdrum gathering for the Society of Long Faces. Festivals were meant to be parties that honored God.

Colossians tells us that there was more to these festivals than what meets the eye. You guessed it — festivals were Old Testament types for Jesus.

> Therefore no one is to act as your judge in regard to food or drink or in respect to a **festival** or a new moon or a **Sabbath** day — things which are a mere **shadow** of what is to come; but the **substance** belongs to **Christ** (Col. 2:16–17).

There is no question that the seven annual festivals are pictures of Jesus and His redemptive work, but caution must be exercised trying to figure out how exactly the festivals foreshadowed Jesus.

Four Spring Festivals

The first of the four annual festivals were spring feasts: Passover, Unleavened Bread, First Fruits, and Pentecost. These were celebrations for the harvest of the spring crop, wheat. These were known as the Harvest Festivals.

The first three festivals, Passover, Unleavened Bread, and First Fruits, are very closely linked as they occur successively.

> These are the appointed times of the Lord, holy convocations which you shall proclaim at the times appointed for them. In the first month, on the **fourteenth** day of the month at twilight is the Lord's **Passover**. Then on the **fifteenth** day of the same month there is the **Feast of Unleavened Bread** to the Lord; for seven days you shall eat unleavened bread. On the first day you shall have a holy convocation; you shall not do any laborious work (Lev. 23:4–7).

1. Passover: Fourteenth day of Nissan (March or April), Friday.

This was covered in chapter four, but if you recall, Passover was the celebration of the night God sent the tenth plague to the Egyptians, forcing the Pharaoh to let God's people go.

God threatened to kill the firstborn son of everyone in the land. Unless. Unless they showed faith by sacrificing a lamb and painting the blood around the doorframe of their homes. This lamb was to be special.

> Only an unblemished, spotless lamb was an acceptable sacrifice.
> The lamb was to be selected on "lamb selection day," Monday.
> The lamb would live with its people for a short time, until Friday.
> The lamb was to be sacrificed in Jerusalem on Friday.
> The lamb was to have no broken bones.

How Is Jesus Like the Passover Lamb?

> Jesus was spotless. He never sinned. Ever.
> Jesus likely entered Jerusalem on Monday of Passover week. This was "lamb selection day."
> Jesus dwelt with us for only a short time, 33 years.

> He was sacrificed in Jerusalem on a Friday.
> Unlike most crucifixion victims, none of Jesus' bones were broken.

How Is Jesus Better Than the Passover Lamb?

> A lamb is an ignorant sacrifice. Jesus was not.
> Before the foundation of the world, Jesus submitted to the pre-arranged plan of the Father to be a willing volunteer and not an unwilling victim (Acts 2:23; Luke 22:42).
> The blood of lambs could only cover sins. Jesus' sacrifice forgives sins and cleanses our consciences.
> Lambs only served as a picture of the Lamb of God who takes away the sins of the world.

Clean out the old **leaven** so that you may be a new lump, just as you are in fact unleavened. For **Christ our Passover** also has been sacrificed (1 Cor. 5:7).

2. Unleavened Bread: Fifteenth Day of Nissan, Saturday

The festival of Unleavened Bread occurred after Passover night, when all the Egyptian firstborn died. The Jews were to bake unleavened bread, a yeast-free flat bread that was quick and easy to make. They were also to purge their homes of leaven.

Once again, this festival was symbolism that served as a reminder of God's faithfulness to His chosen people.

> "They baked the dough which they had brought out of Egypt into cakes of **unleavened bread**. For it had not become leavened, since they were driven out of Egypt and could not delay, nor had they prepared any provisions for themselves" (Exod. 12:39).

> "It is a night to be observed for the LORD for having brought them out from the land of Egypt; this night is for the LORD, to be observed by all the sons of Israel throughout their generations" (Exod. 12:42).

> Leaven was a symbol for sin. The house was to be symbolically purged of sin. This represented God's desire for His people to be holy and set apart.

Paul wrote this to the wayward Corinthian church, fifteen hundred years later:

> "Your boasting is not good. Do you not know that a little **leaven leavens** the whole lump of dough? Clean out the old leaven so that you may be a new lump, just as you are in fact **unleavened**. For **Christ our Passover** also has been sacrificed." (1 Cor. 5:6–7).

The Feast of Unleavened Bread finds its fulfillment in Jesus who is the Passover Lamb who cleanses us from sin. As believers, we are to be "unleavened" from our sin.

First Fruits: Sixteenth of Nissan, Sunday

This feast was a thank offering to God as they offered the first ripe sheaf of barley to the Lord to thank Him for the great harvest to come. This offering was called the First Fruits.

> Then the LORD spoke to Moses, saying, "Speak to the sons of Israel and say to them, 'When you enter the land which I am going to give to you and reap its harvest, then you shall bring in the sheaf of the **first fruits** of your harvest to the priest. He shall **wave the sheaf** before the LORD for you to be accepted; on the day after the Sabbath the priest shall wave it. Now on the day when you wave the sheaf, you shall offer a **male lamb** one year old **without defect** for a burnt offering to the LORD' " (Lev. 23:9–12).

The Shadowy First Fruit Celebration

> One sheaf, the first to represent many more sheaves, was to be raised and waved as the first fruit of many more to come.
> A young, unblemished male lamb was to be sacrificed.

Jesus Is the First fruit

> But now Christ has been **raised** from the dead, the **first fruits** of those who are asleep (1 Cor. 15:20).

On the very day that the first fruit sheaf was to be raised as a sign of many to follow, so Jesus was raised from the dead and is the first of many to follow. This is made clear in 1 Corinthians 15 as Paul stresses the importance of the resurrection from the dead.

> Now if Christ is preached, that He has been **raised** from the dead, how do some among you say that there is no resurrection

of the dead? But if there is no **resurrection** of the dead, not even Christ has been **raised**; and if Christ has not been **raised**, then our preaching is vain, your faith also is vain.

Moreover we are even found to be false witnesses of God, because we testified against God that He **raised** Christ, whom He did not **raise**, if in fact the dead are not **raised**. For if the dead are not **raised**, not even Christ has been **raised**; and if Christ has not been **raised**, your faith is **worthless**; you are still in your sins. Then those also who have fallen asleep in Christ have perished. If we have hoped in Christ in this life only, we are of all men most to be **pitied** (1 Cor. 15:12–19).

The Christian faith is founded on this chief doctrine: Jesus Christ rose from the dead, and if you are in Christ, you will too. If Jesus didn't rise from the dead, we are fools and should be pitied. But He did and we will.

The Festival of First Fruits pictured the Resurrection of Jesus and the resurrection of many to follow. Eyewitnesses testify to it, and we celebrate it every year on Easter Sunday, the same day as the Festival of First Fruits.

4. Feast of Weeks, Known as Pentecost

The fourth festival was called the Festival of Weeks. This festival was to take place 50 days after the Festival of First Fruits.

You shall also count for yourselves from the day after the Sabbath, from the day when you brought in the sheaf of the wave offering; there shall be **seven** complete Sabbaths. You shall count **fifty days** to the day after the seventh Sabbath; then you shall present a new grain offering to the LORD (Lev. 23:15–16).

By the time of Jesus, the Festival of Weeks was referred to as Pentecost, which is the Greek word for "fifty." Today, Jews call this festival "Shavout."

The Festival of Weeks was the summer harvest festival dedicating the future harvest from God. Matthew Henry points out that by Jesus' time, the Festival of Weeks/Pentecost was a festival that celebrated the giving of the Law to Moses and the Jews.[1]

What happened 50 days after Jesus rose from the dead on the Festival of First Fruits?

---

1. "Acts 2:1" from *An Exposition of the Old and New Testaments by Matthew Henry (1708–1710)*; also known as *Matthew Henry's Commentary of the Whole Bible*, http://www.biblestudy-tools.com/commentaries/matthew-henry-complete/.

> When the day of **Pentecost** [Feast of Weeks] had come, they were all together in one place. And suddenly there came from heaven a noise like a violent rushing wind, and it filled the whole house where they were sitting. And there appeared to them tongues as of fire distributing themselves, and they rested on each one of them. And they were all filled with the Holy Spirit and began to speak with other tongues, as the Spirit was giving them utterance (Acts 2:1–4).

Jesus fulfilled His promise to provide His Holy Spirit who is able to help us keep the Law.

Fall Festivals

The three fall festivals are: Feast of Trumpets, Atonement, and Tabernacles. These three festivals happen over 21 days in the fall to celebrate the fall harvests of olives, dates, and figs. These were known collectively as the Tabernacles.

5. The Feast of Trumpets: First day of the Seventh Month

> Again the Lord spoke to Moses, saying, "Speak to the sons of Israel, saying, 'In the seventh month on the first of the month you shall have a rest, a reminder by **blowing of trumpets**, a holy convocation. You shall not do any laborious work, but you shall present an offering by fire to the Lord'" (Lev. 23:23–25).

This was a holy convocation commemorated with trumpet blasts. Again, caution needs to be practiced when it comes to applying the meaning to the festival types, but it seems that the key to our understanding is found in the blowing of the trumpets.

Numbers 10 gives us the biblical significance of trumpet blowing.

> When you go to war in your land against the adversary who attacks you, then you shall sound an alarm **with the trumpets**, that you may be remembered before the Lord your God, and be saved from your enemies. Also in the day of your gladness and in your appointed feasts, and on the first days of your months, you shall **blow the trumpets** over your burnt offerings, and over the sacrifices of your peace offerings; and they shall be as a reminder of you before your God. I am the Lord your God (Num. 10:9–10).

Is it possible that the Feast of Trumpets is a foreshadowing of the return of Jesus?

> [Jesus said,] "And then the sign of the **Son of Man** will appear in the sky, and then all the tribes of the earth will mourn, and they will see the Son of Man coming on the clouds of the sky with **power** and great **glory**. And He will send forth His angels with a great trumpet and they will gather together His elect from the four winds, from one end of the sky to the other" (Matt. 24:30–31).

> Behold, I tell you a mystery; we will not all sleep, but we will all be changed, in a moment, in the twinkling of an eye, at the **last trumpet**; for the trumpet will sound, and the dead will be raised imperishable, and we will be changed (1 Cor. 15:51–52).

> For the Lord Himself will descend from heaven with a shout, with the voice of the archangel and with the **trumpet of God**, and the dead in Christ will rise first (1 Thess. 4:16).

Perhaps the Feast of Trumpets was a foreshadowing of Jesus which has not yet been fulfilled, but will be fulfilled by Him when He returns to earth for Judgment Day.

6. The Day of Atonement: Yom Kippur, Tenth Day of Seventh Month

> The Lord spoke to Moses, saying, "On exactly the **tenth day of this seventh month** is the day of atonement; it shall be a holy convocation for you, and you shall humble your souls and present an offering by fire to the Lord. You shall not do any work on this same day, for it is a **day of atonement**, to make atonement on your behalf before the Lord your God (Lev. 23:26–28).

The high priest was to present two male goats. The first was sacrificed for the nation's sins.

> He [the high priest] shall take the **two goats** and present them before the Lord at the doorway of the tent of meeting. Aaron shall cast lots for the two goats, one lot for the Lord and the other lot for the **scapegoat**. Then Aaron shall offer the goat on which the lot for the Lord fell, and make it a **sin offering** (Lev. 16:7–9).

Jesus is our sin offering (Rom. 8:3). But Jesus is also the second goat on the Day of Atonement.

> But the goat on which the lot for the **scapegoat** fell shall be presented alive before the LORD, to make **atonement** upon it, to send it into the **wilderness** as the scapegoat (Lev. 16:10).

Jesus, our scapegoat, was crucified outside of the city.

> For the bodies of those animals whose blood is brought into the holy place by the high priest as an offering for sin, are burned **outside the camp**. Therefore **Jesus also**, that He might sanctify the people through His own blood, suffered **outside the gate** [of the city of Jerusalem] (Heb. 13:11–12).

Jesus plays a dual role in the symbolism of the Day of Atonement. In ignominy, Jesus was crucified outside of the city that we might be shameless.

7. The Feast of Tabernacles or Booths: Fifteenth through Twenty-third Day of the Seventh Month

> Again the LORD spoke to Moses, saying, "Speak to the sons of Israel, saying, 'On the fifteenth of this seventh month is the **Feast of Booths** for seven days to the LORD. On the first day is a holy convocation; you shall do no laborious work of any kind. For **seven days** you shall present an offering by fire to the LORD. On the **eighth day** you shall have a holy convocation and present an offering by fire to the LORD; it is an assembly. You shall do no laborious work (Lev. 23:33–36).

To commemorate God's faithfulness and supernatural provision during the 40 years of wandering in the wilderness, the Jews were to live in tents (tabernacles/booths) for seven days and then hold a sacred assembly on day eight (Num. 29:35).

Jesus became flesh and "tented" among us (John 1:14). Presently we are the temples of the Holy Spirit (1 Cor. 6:19–20). In the future, at Christ's Second Coming, He will again "tabernacle" with those who are His.

> And I heard a loud voice from the throne, saying, "Behold, the tabernacle of God is among men, and He will **dwell** among them, and they shall be His people, and God Himself will be among them (Rev. 21:3).

The Last Great Day of the Feast of Tabernacles/Booths: Day Eight

Each morning of the feast, at the time of the sacrifice, the priests would draw water in a golden vessel from the pool of Siloam and carry it to the temple to be poured out. This commemorated the water God gave the Jews in the wilderness and served as a symbol that when Messiah comes, the whole world will know God as "water covers the earth" (Isa. 11:9).

Don't miss this picture. During the last great day of the festival, while this elaborate, holy, symbolic gesture was happening, Jesus did something shocking. Again.

> Now on the **last day**, the great day of the feast, Jesus stood and cried out, saying, If anyone is **thirsty**, let him come to Me and **drink**. He who believes in **Me**, as the Scripture said, "From his innermost being will flow rivers of **living water**" (John 7:37–38).

Talk about chutzpah — Jesus was basically saying, "What you are doing is a picture of ME."

Did the Jews understand what Jesus was saying? Upon hearing Jesus' words, some responded by confessing that He was the Messiah, others doubted and some wanted to kill Him (John 7:41–44).

If that weren't enough, what happens next has to be one of the most powerful scenes in the entire Bible.

The Light of the World

During the seven-day celebration of the Feast of Booths, torches were lit to illuminate Jerusalem. The number of lights increased each day so that by day eight on the feast day, Jerusalem was lit up like a rocket. On this day, men carried torches around the temple and placed them in the ground.

This light was to be a symbol of the Messiah who would be a light to the Gentile nations (Isa. 49:6). Jerusalem was ablaze. In the midst of this, with Jerusalem lit up like a comet, Jesus proclaimed:

> I am the **Light of the world**; he who follows Me will not walk in the darkness, but will have the **Light of life**" (John 8:12).

Zing. Pow. Lights out.

While the Jews were festively celebrating with torches blazing everywhere, Jesus' words were absolutely bodacious. "Hey. Those torches you are carrying? The light they give is a picture of Me. You think Jerusalem is a bright light? I am the light of the world!"

Seven hundred years before Jesus began His ministry, the prophet Isaiah predicted, "The people who walk in darkness will see a great **light**; those who live in a dark land, the **light** will shine on them" (Isa. 9:2).

The prophet was right — a great light shined in Israel: "In Him was life, and the life was the **Light of men** (John 1:4). Unfortunately, the darkness did not understand who Jesus was: "The **Light** shines in the darkness, and the darkness did not comprehend it" (John 1:5).

Jesus came and dwelt with His people. He was Immanuel, "God with us." Seven hundred years before Jesus was born to a virgin named Mary, the prophet Isaiah predicted:

> Therefore the Lord Himself will give you a sign: Behold, a virgin will be with child and bear a son, and she will call His name **Immanuel** (Isa. 7:14).

There He was, God with them, and the Jews rejected Him. Shockingly, people did not understand what Jesus, the Light of the World, was saying to them. They did not connect the obvious dots from the old covenant to Him. They were blind and could not see.

You Are Walking in the Light

God has opened your eyes and you have seen the Light. You have repented and placed your faith in the Light of the World, Jesus. Just like the Jews who were given permission to celebrate God at seven festivals, Christians have the supreme reason to celebrate and have joy. Every day.

Joy vs. Happiness

Happiness is nice, but it is fleeting, flimsy, and false. It can never bring lasting, profound joy because its source is shaky.

The world offers happiness through three things:

1. People
2. Places
3. Things

Here's what the world's offer sounds like:

1. If you have a great spouse, you will be happy.
2. If you hang out at interesting places, you will be happy.
3. If you just purchase a _____, you will be happy.

To be sure, the stuff of the world brings happiness, but it is a fleeting feeling.

1. People are sinners and people will disappoint. Babies are a blessing, but happiness is not a word that springs to mind when you are changing your nine thousandth diaper. Spouses are wonderful, but they can do wicked things. You know that if you have been married for at least a day.
2. Places are interesting, but even Tuscany is mundane for the people who get to live there every day.
3. Purchases rust, bust, or break down. That new car smell makes you happy, but it only lasts until your teenager rides shotgun with his shoes off while eating Taco Bell. Houses are great, but unless you love mowing the lawn, and dusting, and cleaning, and repairing, and painting, and replacing roofs, the happiness factor is about a zero on a scale of one to ten.

Happiness is nice, but joy is better. God offers a joy that is profound, lasting and true.

> For the kingdom of God is not eating and drinking, but righteousness and peace and **joy** in the Holy Spirit (Rom. 14:17).

> You will make known to me the path of life;
> In Your presence is fullness of **joy**;
> In Your right hand there are pleasures forever (Ps. 16:11).

We have everlasting joy not because of what people do for us, but because of what God has done for us.

> The LORD has done great things for us; we are **glad** (Ps. 126:3).

And though you have not seen Him, you love Him, and though you do not see Him now, but believe in Him, you greatly rejoice with **joy inexpressible** and full of glory, obtaining as the outcome of your faith the salvation of your souls (1 Pet. 1:8–9).

The Christian life is marked by joy.

> But the fruit of the Spirit is love, **joy**, peace, patience, kindness, goodness, faithfulness, gentleness, self control (Gal. 5:22–23).

Knowing that, the Christian can have joy even when life is hard.

> Consider it **all joy**, my brethren, when you encounter various
> trials, knowing that the testing of your faith produces endurance.
> And let endurance have its perfect result, so that you may be perfect
> and complete, lacking in nothing (James 1:2–4).

The world offers happiness and God offers joy. If you are in Christ, you have
a joy unspeakable.

You Are Walking in Darkness

If you have not repented and trusted, the best thing you will ever experience
is fleeting happiness. Will you continue to stumble in the dark following
the Prince of Darkness? Or will you respond to the Light of the World by
repenting and placing your trust in Him?

Jesus wants you to have joy.

> These things I have spoken to you so that **My joy** may be in
> you, and that **your joy** may be made full (John 15:11).

Did you catch that? Jesus wants you to have the joy that He has. Jesus is the
God of joy. He is not a crabby, curmudgeonly old man in the sky. He wants
you to have joy because He is joy.

Why are you settling for the lesser thing?

250	⊙
	↦ A.D. 33: Jesus crucified
	↦ A.D. 30: Jesus begins ministry
	↦ A.D. 26: John the Baptist begins preaching
0	⊙ 0: Jesus is born
	↦ 397–5 B.C.: The silent years
250	⊙
	↦ 397 B.C.: Malachi is Israel's last prophet until John the Baptist
500	⊙ ↦ 515 B.C.: Jerusalem rebuilt and temple completed
	↦ 536 B.C.: Jews start returning to Jerusalem
	↦ 586 B.C.: Southern Kingdom falls to Babylon
750	⊙ ↦ 721 B.C.: Northern Kingdom falls to Assyria
	↦ 975 B.C.: Israel split in two
1000	⊙ ↦ 1004 B.C.: Solomon's temple completed
	↦ 1015 B.C.: Solomon becomes king
	↦ 1055 B.C.: David becomes king
1250	⊙
	↦ 1451 B.C.: The Jews enter the Promised Land
	↦ 1491–1451 B.C.: The Jews wander the desert
1500	⊙ ↦ 1491 B.C.: Moses leads the Exodus out of Egypt
	↦ 1700–1574 B.C.: Joseph and his brothers have lots of babies
	↦ 1739 B.C.: Joseph sold into slavery in Egypt
1750	⊙
	↦ 1836 B.C.: Jacob born
	↦ 1896 B.C.: Isaac born
2000	⊙ ↦ 1996 B.C. Abraham born
2250	⊙
	↦ 2349 B.C.: Noah and the Global Flood
2500	⊙
2750	⊙
3000	⊙
3250	⊙
3500	⊙
3750	⊙
4000	⊙
	↦ 4004 B.C.: Creation, Adam and Eve, Cain and Abel

Timeline
4004 B.C. — A.D. 33

> *There is no greater sin than misrepresenting God and His Word.*

A GOOD TEACHER

Chapter 15

The Offices of Jesus

Some things never change. The Jews wandered the desert for 40 years (Num. 14:34). Please note, they did not find their way to the Promised Land because Moses pulled over and asked for directions. Typical male.

It was God who finally gave the green light for the Jews to enter the "land flowing with milk and honey" (Exod. 33:3), but only after the rebellious generation had died (Num. 14:35).

Everything that we have already focused on in the Old Testament occurred from the first book (Genesis) through the fifth book (Deuteronomy). These five books, authored by Moses, are known as the Pentateuch (five books) and span the years between 4000 B.C. and 1400 B.C.

The rest of the Old Testament is mostly a history of the nation of Israel in the Promised Land. As you read through the Old Testament, remember, you are seeing the results of the Abrahamic and Mosaic covenants.

God wanted Israel to be a set-apart nation that would produce the Savior of the world. When the Jews were disobedient and unfaithful to the Mosaic

Covenant, God promised to punish them by having a warring neighbor hassle them. When we see God rescuing them, it is because God is faithful to fulfill His promises in the Abrahamic covenant.

The Big Picture

Remember, the Old Testament is not merely a history book. It is a history book with theology that records God's faithfulness to the covenant He cut with Abraham to provide a land, nation and seed.

If you fail to remember that the Old Testament is a story of God's faithfulness to His chosen people so a Messiah could be raised up from a set-apart nation, you will be mislead by preachers who use Old Testament *descriptions* of events and turn them into *prescriptions*. Here is an example.

A Typical Bad Sermon

In the middle of the fifth century B.C., the Jews were under the rule of the Persians. Jerusalem was in shambles. The Prophet Ezra was given permission to rebuild the temple, but the city of Jerusalem was without a wall, leaving it very vulnerable.

> The remnant there in the province who survived the captivity are in great distress and reproach, and **the wall** of Jerusalem is **broken down** and its gates are burned with fire (Neh. 1:3).

In the meantime, a Jew named Nehemiah had a bittersweet job in Persia. He was the king's cupbearer. That meant he had the awesome/scary job of tasting the king's food before the king consumed the meal. This was awesome because Nehemiah was allowed to nibble great food. It was also scary because the food could kill you if someone was trying to poison the king.

Nehemiah had daily access to the king, and he developed a relationship with the most powerful man in the world. Because Nehemiah was grieved over the state of his beloved Jerusalem (Neh. 1:4), he prayed fervently and summoned up the courage to ask the king of Persia if he could return to Jerusalem to build a wall. Permission was remarkably granted and Nehemiah returned to Jerusalem to build a fortified wall around the city.

Countless sermons from this story have had titles like:

> Be a Nehemiah leader!
> Pray like Nehemiah!
> Be a wall builder!

Are there lessons in the Book of Nehemiah on leadership? Perhaps, but that is hardly the point of the story. The Book of Nehemiah was written and recorded to show God's faithfulness to His promise to Abraham that there would always be a land, nation, and seed.

The Jews in Israel had failed to heed the warnings of the Mosaic covenant. Because of their disobedience, God delivered on His promise to punish the Jews for their lack of faithfulness to the Mosaic covenant (Deut. 28). The historical details of Nehemiah are recorded to show God's miraculous delivery of the captive Jews in order to fulfill His promises contained in the Abrahamic covenant.

To read the Book of Nehemiah for leadership lessons is like reading *A Tale of Two Cities* to learn how to be a good lawyer. It's like reading *Moby Dick* to discover fishing tips. It's like reading *The Hobbit* for advice on dealing with hairy feet. It misses the point.

The history of the Old Testament is to demonstrate God's faithfulness to both the Mosaic and Abrahamic covenants. Punishment and redemption are the perpetual themes.

After the Jews entered the Promised Land, we see God's faithfulness over and over again. We also learn how the nation of Israel was governed; God used three offices to govern His people. These too are pictures of Jesus.

Three Offices

The three main offices of the Old Testament were: prophet, priest, and king.

When the Jews entered Canaan, soon to be renamed Israel, God ruled the people directly though a judge. Theocracy (God-rule) is the ideal form of government; you can't do better than to have God as your leader.

Unfortunately, the Jews tired of having "just a judge" and clamored to have a king like the other nations, demonstrating that peer pressure is nothing new. Despite God's warnings that kings will disappoint, the Jews insisted and God granted their request.

God used prophets to preach directly to the people or to instruct the king. Sometimes the king listened, most times he did not.

God also raised up prophets during the Jewish captivities in Assyria and Babylon (for example, Daniel and Ezekiel) as well as prophets after the exile (Ezra and Nehemiah). In other words, prophets were a big deal as they were the "voice of God."

The Prophet's Job

The prophet had one job: to proclaim the Word of the Lord. The prophet would hear from God in an audible or inaudible voice or dream and instruct the people or the king. Usually the "Word of the Lord" was a present command from God, but sometimes the prophets were given a peek into the future and could declare a future event.

Nasty Consequences

If the prophet inaccurately predicted the future, he was to be stoned to death (Deut. 18:22). While that seems severe, there is no greater sin than to claim to speak for God when you do not.

Did you catch that? There is no greater sin than misrepresenting God and His Word. Think of the most heinous crime imaginable and that is not nearly as horrific as mangling God's Word or falsely speaking for Him. This is why false teachings and false teachers are still an abomination to God.

If you are following someone who has unsuccessfully predicted the future, you should run from that person and shout while looking back, "You are lucky this isn't the Old Testament or you would be stoned to death as a false prophet."

While prophets were occasionally given the ability to do a sign or wonder (Moses, Elijah, Elisha), the ultimate proof that a prophet was truly a man of God was his ability to predict the future.

> When a prophet speaks in the name of the Lord, if the thing does not come about or come true, that is the thing which the Lord has not spoken. The prophet has spoken it **presumptuously**; you shall not be afraid of him (Deut. 18:22).

> The prophet who prophesies of peace, when the word of the prophet comes to pass, then that prophet will be known as one whom the Lord has **truly** sent" (Jer. 28:9).

> So when it comes to pass — as surely it will — then they will know that a prophet has been in their midst" (Ezek. 33:33).

David Blaine and David Copperfield can perform great illusions, but the only one who can accurately predict the future is God Himself. The sure test to know if a man was a true or false prophet was the accuracy of his predictions.

Modern-day False Prophets

The list of so-called prophets who have wrongly predicted the future is seemingly endless:

> Joseph Smith, founder of the Mormon Church, predicted that Jesus would return in 56 years. Joseph Smith made that prediction in 1835.[1] Let's see: 1,835 plus 50 = stoning.

> Ellen G. White, founder of the Seventh-day Adventists, predicted the end of the world would occur in 1843. And 1844. And 1845. And 1851. She should have been called, "Out," after her first strike.

> Charles Taze Russell, founder of Jehovah's Witnesses, made many false predictions in the six-volume set, *Studies in the Scriptures*, including the end of the world in 1915. Even if you are bad with dates, you will notice 1915 has come and gone.

> Mary Baker Eddy, founder of the Christian Science cult, made more predictions than Nostradamus. The official Christian Science site lists one of her failed prophecies made in 1891, "The reason for asking, 'Is the Universe, Including Man, Evolved by Atomic Force?' is that Christian Science must answer that question to the world or all will be destroyed by fire in the year 2000."[2]

Even Y2K didn't happen in 2000, let alone the entire planet destroyed by fire. If you follow Mary Baker Eddy, you are following a false prophet.

> David Koresh predicted the world would end in 1995. His world ended in 1992 when the federal government set the Branch Davidian compound on fire.

> Benny Hinn predicted that Fidel Castro would die before the year 2000. Duck, Benny, duck.

> Harold Camping disgracefully predicted the world would come to an end so many times that even he ultimately admitted he had no idea what he was talking about. When he

1. Joseph Smith, *History of the Church of Jesus Christ of Latter-Day Saints*, Vol. 2 (Salt Lake City: Desert News, 1904), p. 189.
2. http://www.christianscience.org/index.php/prophecy/169-predictions-by-mary-baker-eddy.

biffed not once, but twice in 2011 alone, the *New York Times* reported, "Mr. Camping conceded that he had been wrong about the timing and had no evidence that the world would end soon. He offered an apology for his erroneous statements."[3] Oops.

> There are a slew of so-called "New Apostles" (Paul Cain, Bob Jones, John Paul Jackson, Jim Goll, Mike Bickle, Bill Johnson) whose false prophecies are so verifiably false, even they admit they goof. Mike Bickle is on record saying:

> Bob Jones was told that the general level of prophetic revelation in the church was about **65% accurate** at this time. Some are only about 10% accurate, a very few of the most mature prophets are approaching 85% to 95% accuracy. Prophecy is increasing in purity, but there is a still a **long way to go** for those who walk in this ministry. This is actually grace for the church now, because 100% accuracy in this ministry would bring a level of accountability to the church which she is too immature to bear at this time. It would result in too many Ananiases and Saphiras.[4]

That's funny; Ananias and Saphira were killed by God for lying (Acts 5:1–11).

> "Now, obviously, probably **about 80%** of what's in the Body of Christ that's called prophecy is **fleshiness**. And so we're in a day when we're in such an immature stage of this. So much of what is called prophecy is not truly prophecy. So we realize that; so what's our reaction to that? We don't throw out the baby with the bath water. We say, "Lord, we don't throw out prophecy. We ask You to mature it." We don't take it as serious in the early days as we will in the days to come."[5]

Throw out the baby with the bathwater? A 20 percent accuracy rate is closer to a stillborn in a sludge. These wolves make it sound like God has lowered His standard for prophets. He hasn't.

> If a prophet or a **dreamer of dreams** arises among you and gives you a sign or a wonder, and the sign or the wonder **comes**

3. *New York Times*, Dec.17, 2013.
4. Rick Joyner, "The Prophetic Ministry," *Morningstar Prophetic Newsletter*, vol. 3, no. 2, p. 2.
5. Albert James Dager, "The Restoration of Apostles and Prophets and the Kansas City-Vineyard Connection," *Media Spotlight*, September 1990.

true, concerning which he spoke to you, saying, "Let us go after other gods (whom you have not known) and let us serve them," you shall not listen to the words of that prophet or that dreamer of dreams; for the LORD your **God is testing you** to find out if you love the LORD your God with all your heart and with all your soul.

You shall follow the LORD your God and fear Him; and you shall keep His commandments, listen to His voice, serve Him, and cling to Him. But that **prophet or that dreamer of dreams shall be put to death**, because he has counseled rebellion against the LORD your God who brought you from the land of Egypt and redeemed you from the house of slavery, to seduce you from the way in which the LORD your God commanded you to walk. So you shall **purge the evil** from among you (Deut. 13:1–5).

Run from false prophets and watch for flying rocks as you go.

Jesus Is the Greatest Prophet

The people who heard Jesus preach and watched Him perform miracles knew He was a prophet. That is why the two men who walked with the resurrected Jesus on the road to Emmaus said Jesus the Nazarene was "a prophet mighty in deed and word in the sight of God and all the people" (Luke 24:19).

In a sense, all of the Old Testament prophets were minor prophets who served as a type of the major prophet to come, Jesus Christ.

Jesus Predicted the Future Accurately

And again He took the twelve aside and began to tell them **what was going to happen** to Him, saying, "Behold, we are going up to Jerusalem, and the Son of Man will be delivered to the chief priests and the scribes; and they will condemn Him to death and will hand Him over to the Gentiles. They will mock Him and spit on Him, and scourge Him and kill Him, and three days later He will rise again" (Mark 10:32–34).

Now that is specific and accurate. Jesus' prediction was fulfilled perfectly.

Jesus Performed Miracles

Not only did Jesus perform miracles like Old Testament prophets, He performed more and greater miracles than all of them. Combined.

> Jesus healed thousands of sick people (Acts 10:38).
> Jesus fed thousands of people from a few loaves of bread and a few fish (Matt. 14:13–21).
> Jesus walked on water (Matt. 14:22–33).
> Jesus calmed the storm (Mark 4:35-41).
> Jesus raised people from the dead (John 11:1–44).
> Jesus raised Himself from the dead (John 2:19–22).

Priest

The office of priest is a story line that weaves its way throughout the entire Bible. They were in charge of the temple, God's holy place, to offer sacrifices, take care of the poor, and act as the mediator between man and God.

Many priests worked in the temple, but the high priest was the chief of all priests. This was the priest who annually entered the Holy of Holies in the temple to sprinkle the blood of a lamb on God's mercy seat for the covering of the nations' sins.

Jesus Is Our Great High Priest

But when Christ appeared as a **high priest** of the good things to come, He entered through the **greater** and more perfect tabernacle, not made with hands, that is to say, not of this creation; and not through the blood of goats and calves, but through **His own blood**, He entered the holy place **once for all**, having obtained eternal redemption.

For if the blood of goats and bulls and the ashes of a heifer sprinkling those who have been defiled sanctify for the cleansing of the flesh, how much **more** will the blood of Christ, who through the eternal Spirit offered Himself without blemish to God, cleanse your conscience from dead works to serve the living God? (Heb. 9:11–14).

Jesus Is a Better High Priest

> Jesus intercedes for us as He sits next to the Father.
> Jesus offered His own blood, not the blood of an animal.
> Jesus is the sacrifice given once for all time.
> Temple priests were temporary; Jesus is permanent.
> Temple sacrifices were repeated; Jesus' offering happened once.

> Temple sacrifices only offered a picture of forgiveness; Jesus sacrifice provided actual forgiveness.
> Temple sacrifices did not remove guilt, Jesus' sacrifice did.

The former priests, on the one hand, existed in greater numbers because they were prevented by death from continuing, **but Jesus**, on the other hand, because He **continues forever**, holds His priesthood **permanently**. Therefore He is able also to save forever those who draw near to God through Him, since He always lives to make intercession for them.

For it was fitting for us to have such a high priest, holy, innocent, undefiled, separated from sinners and exalted above the heavens; who does not need daily, like those high priests, to offer up sacrifices, first for His own sins and then for the sins of the people, because this He did **once for all** when He **offered up Himself**. For the Law appoints men as high priests who are weak, but the word of the oath, which came after the Law, appoints a Son, made **perfect forever** (Heb. 7:23–28).

Jesus is the highest of all high priests. He is greater than any earthly intercessor. His sacrifice is forever accepted by the Father.

Perseverance of the Saints

If you are in Christ, the great High Priest, His once-and-for-all perfect sacrifice has been credited to your account. You have been granted perfect redemption with complete forgiveness of sins.

Because of the high priestly work of Jesus, your sin debt has been removed. Why would you think for a second you can lose your salvation?

When you were dead in your transgressions and the uncircumcision of your flesh, He made you alive together with Him, having **forgiven us all our transgressions**, **having canceled out the certificate of debt** consisting of decrees against us, which was hostile to us; and He has taken it out of the way, having **nailed it to the cross** (Col. 2:13–14).

All of your sins, past, present, and future have been nailed to the Cross. Why would you think you can un-nail your sins?

The salvation that has been granted to you is perfect. Even you can't wreck it!

When God saves, He saves through the perfect work and sacrifice of Jesus. He will not un-save you. If He has made you a saint (Rom. 1:7), He will keep you a saint.

To those who reside as aliens, scattered throughout Pontus, Galatia, Cappadocia, Asia, and Bithynia, who are **chosen** according to the **foreknowledge** of God the Father, by the sanctifying work of the Spirit, to obey Jesus Christ and be **sprinkled with His blood**: May grace and peace be yours in the fullest measure.

Blessed be the God and Father of our Lord Jesus Christ, who according to His great mercy has **caused us to be born again** to a living hope through the resurrection of Jesus Christ from the dead, to obtain an inheritance which is **imperishable** and **undefiled** and **will not fade away, reserved** in heaven for you, who are protected by the power of God through faith for a salvation ready to be revealed in the last time (1 Pet. 1:1–5).

You cannot get yourself saved; you cannot keep yourself saved; but God has and God will. If you are a professing believer who sometimes feels uncertain of your standing with God, remember, your standing with God is not based on your performance. It is based on the high priestly work of the Great High Priest, the Lord Jesus Christ.

What then shall we say to these things? If God is for us, who is against us? He who did not spare His own Son, but delivered Him over for us all, how will He not also with Him freely give us all things? Who will bring a charge against God's elect? God is the one who justifies; **who is the one who condemns?** Christ Jesus is He who died, yes, rather who was raised, who is at the right hand of God, who also **intercedes for us**. Who will **separate us** from the love of Christ? Will tribulation, or distress, or persecution, or famine, or nakedness, or peril, or sword? Just as it is written,

"For Your sake we are being put to death all day long; We were considered as sheep to be slaughtered."

But in all these things we overwhelmingly **conquer** through Him who loved us. For I am convinced that **neither** death, **nor** life, **nor** angels, **nor** principalities, **nor** things present, **nor** things to come, **nor** powers, **nor** height, **nor** depth, **nor** any other created thing, **will be able** to separate us from the love of God, which is in Christ Jesus our Lord (Rom. 8:31–39).

If you are in Him:

> The devil cannot separate you from the love of God.
> Your spouse cannot separate you from the love of God.
> Your parents cannot separate you from the love of God.
> Accusers cannot separate you from the love of God.
> Your sin cannot separate you from the love of God.
> Your past cannot separate you from the love of God.
> Your weak faith cannot separate you from the love of God.
> Your doubts cannot separate you from the love of God.
> You cannot separate you from the love of God.

You have a Great High Priest, rest in Him.

King

Israel had the best governmental system ever: theocracy. God was their King who ruled through judges who were guided by prophets. But Israel looked around and saw that some of their cool neighbors had kings. So what did they do? They asked God for a king.

> Then all the elders of Israel gathered together and came to Samuel at Ramah; and they said to him, "Behold, you have grown old, and your sons do not walk in your ways. Now **appoint a king for us** to judge **us like all the nations**" (1 Sam. 8:4–5).

The Jews requested a lesser thing, and God, who must have been grieved over their rejection, told Samuel to inform them that He would allow them to have a human king. Notice the horrific consequences of their foolish request.

> So Samuel spoke all the words of the LORD to the people who had asked of him a king. He said, "This will be the procedure of **the king who will reign over you:** he will **take your sons** and place them for himself in his chariots and among his horsemen and they will run before his chariots. He will appoint for himself commanders of thousands and of fifties, and **some to do his plowing** and to reap his harvest and to make his weapons of war and equipment for his chariots.
>
> "**He will also take your daughters** for perfumers and cooks and bakers. He will **take** the best of your fields and your vineyards and your olive groves and give them to his servants. He will **take** a

tenth of your seed and of your vineyards and give to his officers and to his servants.

"He will also **take** your male servants and your female servants and your best young men and your donkeys and use them for his work. He will **take** a tenth of your flocks, and **you yourselves will become his servants**" (1 Sam. 8:10–17).

Then came the granddaddy of all warnings:

"Then you will cry out in that day because of your king whom you have chosen for yourselves, but the LORD **will not answer** you in that day" (1 Sam. 8:18).

God warned them of the consequences of their decision. He could not have been more clear that their desire for a king was going to be a disaster; the king will take your land, labors, and even your children. The Jews had deaf ears. The peer pressure was too great and the children of Israel didn't hear God's warnings.

Nevertheless, the people refused to listen to the voice of Samuel, and they said, "No, but there shall be a king over us, **that we also may be like all the nations**, that our king may judge us and go out before us and fight our battles." Now after Samuel had heard all the words of the people, he repeated them in the LORD's hearing. The LORD said to Samuel, "Listen to their voice and appoint them a king" (1 Sam. 8:19–22).

God was right. Predominantly, the kings of Israel (the ten northern tribes) and Judah (the two southern tribes) "did evil in the sight of the Lord." There was the occasional good king, like David and Josiah, but overall, they were stinkers.

The Promised King

God made a promise to King David that a king from the lineage of David was going to come, and He would reign forever. This is the promise of the Davidic Covenant.

When your days are fulfilled that you must go to be with your fathers, that I **will set up one of your descendants after you**, who will be of your sons; and I will establish **his kingdom**. He shall build for Me a house, and I will establish his **throne forever**. I will be his **father** and he shall be My **son**; and I will not take My lovingkindness away from him, as I took it from him who was before you. But I will settle him in My house and in My kingdom **forever**, and his throne shall be established **forever** (1 Chron. 17:11–14).

Balaam the prophet gave a future prediction of this coming, conquering king.

> I see him, but not now;
> I behold him, but not near;
> A star shall come forth from Jacob,
> A **scepter shall rise from Israel** (Num. 24:17).

The prophet Jeremiah predicted a coming king of Israel.

> "Behold, the days are coming," declares the LORD,
> "When I will raise up for David a righteous Branch;
> And He will reign as **king** and act wisely
> And do justice and righteousness in the land.
> "In His days Judah will be saved,
> And Israel will dwell securely;
> And this is His name by which He will be called,
> '**The Lord our righteousness**' " (Jer. 23:5–6).

Jesus Is the King

The theme of the entire book of the Gospel of Matthew is: Jesus is the King! The Old Testament kings were merely types, shadows of the true, only, and best king, King Jesus.

Matthew uses the genealogy of Jesus to show that He is a descendant of King David (Matt. 1:6). The magi knew that a king was promised. That is why they asked King Herod, "Where is the newborn King of the Jews?" (Matt. 2:2; NLT).

Kings always had heralds who would go before them to prepare the people for the coming king. John the Baptist was the herald of Jesus (Matt. 3:1–3).

Jesus acted like a king when He entered Jerusalem on a donkey.

> This took place to fulfill what was spoken through the prophet:
> "Say to the Daughter of Zion,
> 'Behold, your **king** is coming to you,
> Gentle and mounted on a donkey,
> Even on a colt, the foal of a beast of burden' " (Matt. 21:4–5).

In case anyone was confused that Jesus is King, Matthew made it abundantly clear when Pontius Pilate interrogated Jesus.

> Now Jesus stood before the governor, and the governor questioned Him, saying, "Are You the **King of the Jews**?" And Jesus said to him, "It is as you say" (Matt. 27:11).

Ignorantly, the Roman soldiers who crucified Jesus placed a sign above the crucified King.

> And above His head they put up the charge against Him which read, "THIS IS JESUS THE **KING OF THE JEWS**" (Matt. 27:37).

The Coming King

One day, King Jesus will return. When He does, it will not be on a donkey, it will be on a stallion.

> And I saw heaven opened, and behold, a **white horse**, and He who sat on it is called Faithful and True, and in righteousness He judges and **wages war**. His eyes are a flame of fire, and on His head are many diadems; and He has a name written on Him which no one knows except Himself.
>
> He is clothed with a robe dipped in blood, and His name is called **The Word of God**. And the armies which are in heaven, clothed in fine linen, white and clean, were following Him on white horses.
>
> From His mouth comes a sharp sword, so that with it He may strike down the nations, and He will **rule them** with a rod of iron; and He treads the wine press of the fierce wrath of God, the Almighty.
>
> And on His robe and on His thigh He has a name written, "**KING OF KINGS**, AND LORD OF LORDS" (Rev. 19:11–16).

Murders are committed and the perpetrator goes free. Rapists rape and the justice system cannot find the scoundrel. Child abusers abuse and frighten a child into a lifetime of shameful silence.

One day, soon, King Jesus will return and He will wage war against sinners. He will "pour out the fierce wrath of God" against each and every sinner for each and every sin.

Justice will be executed for every crime committed against man and God. No dirty deed will go unpunished. No filthy act will escape His eye. Every dark activity will be brought into the light.

He who planted the ear, does He not hear?
He who formed the eye, does He not see? (Ps. 94:9).

Not Just Criminals

While you might rejoice that King Jesus is going to deal with the "bad guys," here is the problem: we are all bad guys. You may not think you have committed a really big crime, but all sins are a crime against God and He will seek you out, find you, and bring you into the courtroom of His justice and He will sentence you.

> Or do you not know that the unrighteous will **not inherit** the **kingdom of God**? Do not be deceived; neither fornicators, nor idolaters, nor adulterers, nor effeminate, nor homosexuals, nor thieves, nor the covetous, nor drunkards, nor revilers, nor swindlers, will inherit the **kingdom of God** (1 Cor. 6:9–10).

We are all in trouble, unless we have a perfect prophet, a perfect priest, and a perfect king.

Munus Triplex: Threefold Office

An Old Testament prophet could not hold the office of priest or king. An Old Testament priest could not be a prophet or king. An Old Testament king could not be a priest or prophet.

Jesus Christ was and is all three!

Jesus Christ is the king who submitted Himself to the will of the Father and left His throne to humble Himself and live as a servant (Phil. 2:7) to die for His rebellious subjects.

Jesus Christ is the great High Priest who mediates a new covenant and offers complete and total forgiveness because of His redemptive work.

Jesus Christ is the prophet who rightly predicted the future when He said,

> But when the Son of Man comes in His glory, and all the angels with Him, then He will sit on **His glorious throne**. All the nations will be gathered before Him; and He will separate them from one another, as the shepherd separates the sheep from the goats; and He will put the sheep on His right, and the goats on the left.
>
> Then the **King** will say to those on His right, "**Come, you who are blessed** of My Father, inherit the **kingdom** prepared for you from the foundation of the world" (Matt. 25:31–34).

Then He will also say to those on His left, "**Depart from Me**, accursed ones, into the eternal fire which has been prepared for the devil and his angels. . . ." These will go away into eternal punishment, but the righteous into eternal life (Matt. 25:41–46).

Heed Prophet Jesus' prediction. Today, bow before the King. The great High Priest will apply His redemptive work to you and He will save you "**to the uttermost**" (Heb. 7:25; ESV).

To the Uttermost

What does it mean to be saved "to the uttermost?"

1. Jesus will save the vilest of sinners (Luke 23:40–43).
2. Jesus will forgive all sins, past, present, and future (Col. 2:13–14).
3. Jesus will cleanse your conscience (Heb. 9:13–14).
4. Jesus will give you a new nature (Eph. 4:23, 24; Col. 3:10).
5. Jesus will help you make sense of the world (Rom. 12:2).
6. Jesus will give you hope (Rom. 15:4).
7. Jesus will give you a future (1 Pet. 1:3–5).

Jesus is willing to save you to the uttermost. Would you expect anything less from the King of the universe?

> *Criminals don't go to jail because they cannot pay
> their fine, they go to jail for breaking the law.*

OPTIONAL

Chapter 16

Jesus Is People

Do you know what Adam and Eve did when their son, Cain, killed his brother Abel?

They raised Cain.

Thank you. Thank you very much. Two shows on Saturday, try the veal and trip your waitress.

Perhaps you knew that Abel was the first murder victim in history, but did you know Abel was a prophet who was the first person to be a type of Jesus? God did not waste time after the Fall to give us a picture of the Savior in the form of a person.

The Old Testament lists many people who are shadowy pictures of Jesus. Remember, types are LESSER pictures of the substance, Jesus. We also have to practice caution that we don't ascribe too many details between the shadow and the fulfillment.

Abel

Abel offered a blood sacrifice to God in faith. God was pleased.

Cain gave a faithless grain offering. God was not pleased.

Cain committed the first murder by whacking his brother Abel (Gen. 4:3–8).

Jesus Is Like Abel, Only Better

Hebrews 12:24 tells us that the blood of Jesus speaks of better things than the blood of Abel. The first murder was a fuzzy picture of the most heinous murder of all time.

Jesus, like Abel, was killed by His brothers, His fellow Jews.

Abel's sacrifice of an animal only provided a temporary covering for sins; Jesus' sacrifice provided complete and total forgiveness of sins.

Melchizedek

If you are looking for a unique name for your newborn son, Melchizedek is available. Melchizedek is also an Old Testament type of Jesus.

One day, Abraham was returning from war when he met a king of Salem (ancient Jerusalem) named Melchizedek. While we are not given many details about this fellow, we are told that he was a "priest of God Most High" (Gen. 14:18). Sketchy, very sketchy.

This priest blessed Abraham and Abraham gave him a tenth of his spoils.

This story seems to be inserted without much fanfare and for apparently no reason — until two thousand years later when the author of Hebrews tells us that Jesus is a "priest forever according to the order of Melchizedek" (Heb. 5:6).

As always, Jesus, the substance, is better than the shadow.

> Jesus was not just a priest, but a High Priest (Heb. 4:14).
> Jesus is the guarantee of a better covenant (Heb. 7:22).
> Jesus is not merely the King of Salem but the King of everything (Rev. 1:4–5).
> Genesis does not provide the ancestry or death of Melchizedek, making his priesthood appear eternal. Jesus' priesthood is eternal (Heb. 7:3).

Isaac

This story is told in detail in chapter 4, so you likely recall the details.

> A loving father (Abraham) nearly sacrificed his only beloved son, Isaac (Gen. 22:2).
> Isaac was completely unaware of what was going to happen (Gen. 22:7).
> The location of the sacrifice was Mount Moriah, outside of the city of Jerusalem (Gen. 22:2).
> The son carried wood to the sacrifice (Gen. 22:6).

Isaac Is a Type of Jesus

> God the Father actually sacrificed His only beloved Son, Jesus (John 3:16).
> Jesus knew exactly what was going to happen to Him (John 16:16).
> Jesus was sacrificed outside of the city of Jerusalem (Heb. 13:12), likely on Mount Moriah.
> Jesus carried wood, a Cross, to His sacrifice (John 19:7).

The story of Isaac ends with a beloved Father NOT sacrificing his only beloved son on a mountain outside of Jerusalem. Two thousand years later, when we visit that same mountain, the Father did not stop.

Moses

When Moses died, it was said of him:

> Since that time no prophet has risen in Israel **like Moses**, whom the LORD knew face to face, for all the signs and wonders which the LORD sent him to perform in the land of Egypt against Pharaoh, all his servants, and all his land, and for all the mighty power and for all the great terror which Moses performed in the sight of all Israel (Deut. 34:10–12).

Moses, the greatest prophet of the Old Testament, was predicting the future when he said:

> The LORD your God will raise up for you **a prophet like** me from among you, from your countrymen, you shall listen to him (Deut. 18:15).

Jesus proclaimed Himself to the fulfillment of this prophecy when He said, "For if you believed Moses, you would believe Me, for **he wrote about Me** (John 5:46).

Moses was a servant. Jesus was a servant.

> For even the Son of Man did not come to be served, but to
> **serve**, and to give His life a ransom for many (Mark 10:45).

Moses gave the Law. Jesus magnified the Law in the Sermon on the Mount,
repeatedly saying, "You have heard [from Moses] . . . but I say to you . . ."
(Matt. 5:21, 27, 33, 38, 43).

Moses led the captives to freedom. Jesus purchased our freedom (John
8:31–32).

> And He came to Nazareth, where He had been brought up; and
> as was His custom, He entered the synagogue on the Sabbath, and
> stood up to read. And the book of the prophet Isaiah was handed
> to Him. And He opened the book and found the place where it was
> written,
>
> > "The Spirit of the Lord is upon Me,
> > Because He anointed Me to preach the gospel to the poor.
> > He has sent Me to proclaim release to the captives,
> > And recovery of sight to the blind,
> > To **set free** those who are oppressed,
> > To proclaim the favorable year of the Lord."
>
> And He closed the book, gave it back to the attendant and sat
> down; and the eyes of all in the synagogue were fixed on Him. And
> He began to say to them, "Today this Scripture **has been fulfilled**
> in your hearing" (Luke 4:16–21).

Moses delivered the Jews from slavery and death. Jesus delivers us from the
slavery of sin and death (2 Cor. 1:10).

Moses brought the Jews to the Promised Land. Jesus promises to bring
us to the greater Promised Land.

> In My Father's house are many dwelling places; if it were not so,
> I would have told you; for I go to prepare **a place for you**. If I go
> and prepare a place for you, I will come again and **receive you** to
> Myself, that where I am, *there* you may be also (John 14:2,3).

Jonah

Jesus answered and said to them, "An evil and adulterous generation craves
for a sign; and yet no sign will be given to it but the sign of Jonah the
prophet (Matt. 12:39).

Jonah was a prophet. Jesus was a prophet (Luke 24:19).

Jonah was in the belly of a big fish for three days. Jesus was in the belly of the earth for three days (Matt. 12:39).

Jonah preached repentance. Jesus preached repentance (Mark 1:15).

King Solomon

The son of David, Solomon, was considered the wisest man to ever live. Jesus declared:

> "The Queen of the South will rise up with this generation at the judgment and will condemn it, because she came from the ends of the earth to hear the wisdom of Solomon; and behold, **something greater than Solomon** is here" (Matt. 12:42).

How was Jesus a Solomon type?

> Solomon and Jesus were both from the line of David (Matt. 1:6).
> Solomon and Jesus were both kings (Rev. 19:16).
> Solomon and Jesus were both wise (Luke 2:47; Mark 12:17).
> Solomon built the temple; Jesus built the Church (Matt. 16:18).
> Solomon built a massive physical kingdom; Jesus is building a larger spiritual kingdom (Matt. 16:18).

Other People Who Probably Were Types

Remember, we are using a conservative rule: we can only be sure of Old Testament types and shadows if the New Testament confirms them. Having said that, there are some people who just scream "Jesus-type," even though the New Testament doesn't directly affirm them as a type.

Boaz

In the Book of Ruth, we are shown a concept that was quite common in Israel: the kinsman redeemer (Deut. 25:5–6). A kinsman redeemer would marry the widowed wife of a deceased brother. This was done to keep the brother's name alive.

In the Book of Ruth, we read the story of a poor, pagan widow named Ruth. A loving relative of her deceased husband, Boaz, gladly redeemed her and made her his bride (Ruth 3, 4). He did not redeem her by paying for her, he redeemed her situation and bought her out of poverty to a better life.

Jesus Is a Boaz Type

> Boaz was a loving man. Jesus is supremely loving (1 John 4:8).
> Boaz provided a better physical life. Jesus provides eternal life.
> Boaz redeemed one person. Jesus redeems millions.

Joseph

If any Old Testament person appears to be a "type of Christ" without being affirmed in the New Testament, it is Joseph. To read one of the most gripping and moving stories ever written, read the story of Joseph in Genesis 37 thru 45.

This chart from Andrew Bernhardt's website lists the many, many similarities between Joseph and Jesus.[1] Are all of these comparisons accurate? Maybe. The point is, Joseph sure appears to be a Jesus-type.

Similarities	Joseph	Jesus
Both are first-born.	Genesis 30:22–24 (of Rachel)	Matthew 1:25 (of Mary)
Both are shepherds.	Genesis 37:2	Matthew 2:26, 26:31; John 10:11
Both are the most loved of their fathers.	Genesis 37:3	Matthew 3:17, 12:18
Both were prophesied to be rulers.	Genesis 37:5–11	Daniel 7:13–14; Micah 4:7, 5:2; Psalm 2
Both Joseph's and Jesus' brothers were jealous of them, and did not believe them.	Genesis 37:4–11	John 7:3–5, 15:18–19
The prophecies that Joseph would rule his brothers (the tribes of Israel), and Jesus would rule the whole world, including Israel.	Genesis 37:6–11	Daniel 7:13–14; Psalm 2:1–12
Joseph was sent by his father to his brothers. Jesus was sent by His Father to Israel.	Genesis 37:13, 18–20	Matthew 21:37–38; Mark 12:6–7; Luke 20:13–15; John 5:23
Joseph was apparently put to death, and Jesus truly, by their own people.	Genesis 37:18–28	Acts 2:22–23

---

1. http://dtjsoft.com/joseph-a-type-of-christ/.

Joseph was sold as a slave to Egypt. Jesus was betrayed for the price of a slave.	Genesis 37:26–28	Matthew 26:15; Exodus 21:32; Zechariah 11:12–13
Both went to Egypt.	Genesis 37:28	Matthew 2:13–15
Both were made slaves.	Genesis 39:1	Philippians 2:7
Both were falsely accused.	Genesis 39:11–20	Matthew 26:5–61
God was with them both.	Genesis 39:3, 21, 23; Acts 7:9	Acts 10:38; Luke 2:52; John 1:1–2, 3:2
Both were with two others condemned to die, one of whom was pardoned and given life.	Genesis 40:1–3, 20–22	Luke 23:32, 39–43
God's Spirit indwelt them both.	Genesis 41:38	Luke 4:1; Acts 10:38
All knees bowed to Joseph. All knees will bow to Jesus.	Genesis 41:43	Philippians 2:10
Both were given a Gentile bride by the king.	Genesis 41:45	2 Corinthians 11:2
The king of Egypt appointed Joseph to be the sole source of life for all. God appointed Jesus to be our sole source of eternal life.	Genesis 41:55–57	Acts 4:12; 1 John 5:11–12
Joseph's brothers did not recognize him. Jesus' own people didn't either.	Genesis 42:8	John 1:10
The evil Joseph's brothers intended God meant for good to save them. The same is true of the evil Jesus' own people intended to him.	Genesis 45:5–8, 50:20	Acts 3:12–18
Joseph's brothers shared Pharaoh's favor because of Joseph, not themselves. We share God's favor because of Jesus, not because we are worthy.	Genesis 45:16–20	Ephesians 2:4–8; Philippians 4:19
Both are saviors.	Genesis 47:25	Acts 13:23

The list goes on and on:

> Joseph and Jesus were victorious over temptation (Matt. 4:10–11).
> Joseph and Jesus were bound, condemned, and placed in prison (Mark 15:1; Luke 23:20–25).
> Joseph and Jesus were ultimately exalted (Phil. 2:9–11).

While the New Testament never says that Joseph is a "Jesus-type," it is hard to imagine that he was not.

Adam Is an Anti-type

The first man, Adam, is a type of Jesus, only completely different. An anti-type is a person that is given to be a picture of what the substance is not. Adam is not a type of Christ; he is an anti-type. A type is a comparison; an anti-type is a contrast. Adam and Jesus are contrasted in Romans 5.

Poor Adam

One wonders how long the line in heaven will be to meet the first man, Adam. How many times will he have to say, "I know, I know. I blew it!"

Before we throw a stone at poor old Adam, we might want to put our rocks down for a minute. The Bible makes it clear that you and I would have done no better than Adam at resisting the temptation to eat the forbidden fruit (Rom. 5:12).

Adam was no different than you and me; he was no better and he was no worse. Adam was just a man.

Federal Head

While Adam was a typical fella, he did have one thing we do not: a different role. God made Adam our representative, our federal head. This is not just a Mideastern concoction; you and I have federal heads today.

> Your father represents and speaks for your family. If your father does something shameful, the entire family is tarnished.
> Your governor represents and speaks for your state. He does something dopey and your state is mocked.
> Your president represents and speaks for your country. If your federal head biffs it, the entire nation gets a black eye.

Adam was your federal head and he represented you in the garden. Like it or not (and I lean toward the "not" side), what he did affected all of us.

> Therefore, just as through **one man** sin entered into the world, and death through sin, and so death spread to all men, because **all sinned** (Rom. 5:12).

Adam sinned and you and I get credit. Because Adam sinned, you and I are sinners too. But here is a substantial difference: Adam was created perfect and became a sinner, whereas you and I are born sinners and remain sinners.

We are born "in sin" (Ps. 51:3). We die because of our sin (Rom. 6:23).

> For until the Law sin was in the world, but sin is not imputed when there is no law. Nevertheless **death reigned** from Adam until Moses, even over those who had not sinned in the likeness of the offense of Adam, **who is a type** of Him who was to come (Rom. 5:13–14).

That is a pretty tricky verse. Paul is explaining that between the time of Adam and Moses, there was no law, yet people died. Violation of the law is what brings death, but there was no law and yet people died. Why? Because they were in Adam who was their federal head. Adam became a sinner and because we are in Adam, we are sinners from birth, and the wages of sin is death (Rom. 6:23).

Total Depravity

Humans are conceived in sin (Ps. 51:5). Romans 5 tells us that we are totally depraved. It doesn't mean that everything we do is depraved, it means that everything about us is fallen and sinful from birth. We are born sinful, and left to our totally depraved selves, we will die and go to hell because of our sin.

Some people say that we go to hell because we don't believe in Jesus. That is not exactly correct. We go to hell because of our sins. It is the chief and greatest sin to reject Jesus, but that is just one of our many, many sins.

Why Criminals Go to Jail

If you were pulled over for speeding and given a $200 fine that you could not pay, would you be hauled off to jail because you could not pay the fine or because you broke the law? In a sense it is because you cannot pay, but the actual reason for your arrest is because you have committed a crime.

Criminals don't go to jail because they cannot pay their fine, they go to jail for breaking the law.

If we never broke a law, we would never go to jail. If we never sinned we would not go to hell and we would not need the forgiveness that is found in Jesus. But we do break God's laws and that is why we go to hell. It also happens to be a violation of God's law to not believe on His Son.

Sinners go to hell because they sin. Lawbreakers go to hell because they break the laws. Humans do not go to hell because their fines are not paid, they go to hell because they are guilty criminals who have broken God's laws.

Conversely, Christians go to heaven because their fine has been paid and their sins have been forgiven.

Babies

Perhaps you are wondering about babies. If babies are born sinners and they die, do they go to hell? The answer is a thunderous, "NO!" Babies who die go to heaven. Period.

Perhaps you are thinking that contradicts what you just read. If humans are born sinners and sinners go to hell, then babies, who are born sinners, should go to hell. While that seems logical, there is a piece of missing information that changes that equation.

Babies do not sin against God willfully.

Yes, babies sin, but they do not do it with the knowledge that they are rebelling against God. A child from birth until a certain age commits pretty much every sin imaginable, but he does so without knowledge.

Safe in the Arms of God is a wonderfully comforting book by Dr. John MacArthur, who lays out the biblical case that babies go to heaven. Here are just ten of the verses he assembled to prove that babies are wicked little sinners who do not have their sins credited to them because they don't know "their right hand from their left."

1. In Jonah 4:11, God refers to the children of pagan Nineveh as not "knowing their right hand from their left," meaning, they don't know the difference between good and evil.
2. In Ezekiel 16:21, the Lord calls the children of pagans "My children."
3. In Deuteronomy 1:39, God makes it clear that children "have no knowledge of good and evil."
4. In Jeremiah 19:4, murdered children of pagans are called "innocents" by God.
5. In Job 3:16–19, Job declares unequivocally that dead infants do not go to hell. They go to heaven.

6. In 2 Samuel 12:23, David proclaims that he will see his dead infant son in heaven.
7. Isaiah 7:16 describes an age where children learn the difference between good and evil.
8. In Matthew 2 and 3, Jesus describes the kingdom of heaven as made up of those who are like "little children." This analogy only makes sense if little children actually are in heaven.
9. In Matthew 18:3–5, Jesus blessed the little children. Jesus never blessed anyone who was rebelling against Him.
10. Revelation 5:10 tells us that "every tribe and tongue" will be represented in heaven. As many tribes no longer exist, this verse must be describing children as included in the myriad who will be praising God.

Level of Accountability

The Bible is clear — a child is innocent before God, even though they sin, because they have not reached an age where they are accountable to God for their actions. Some people use the term, "age of accountability," but it is best to use the term, "level of accountability," as each child matures at different rates.

For many cultures and religions, that approximate age has been associated with puberty. Jewish bar and bat mitzvahs, Lutheran confirmation and African passage ceremonies from boyhood to manhood happen at this time.

Once a child reaches a level where he understands that sin is willful rebellion, in other words, when he knows better, then he is accountable to God. If he dies in his sin having reached a level of accountability, he will be sentenced by God as a guilty criminal. Prior to that level, God welcomes that little one to heaven.

People with Intellectual Disability

God is not mean. God is not eager to send people to hell. God is eager to save; that is why He sent His Son to earth. God saves people who do not have the mental capacity to comprehend the sinfulness of their sin. God takes those who "don't know their right hand from their left" to heaven, regardless of their age.

Bad News

If you are reading this book, it is likely that you are at a level of accountability to comprehend your sin and guilt. As a child of Adam, you are totally depraved and in terrible trouble, unless a Second Adam comes.

Good News

The first Adam blew it. The Second Adam did not.

> **But** the free gift is not like the transgression. For if by the trans-
> gression of **the one the many died**, much more did the grace of
> God and the gift by the **grace of the one Man**, Jesus Christ, abound
> to the many. The gift is not like that which came through the **one**
> **who sinned**; for on **the one hand** the judgment arose from one
> transgression resulting in condemnation, but on **the other hand** the
> free gift arose from many transgressions resulting in justification.
> For if by the transgression of **the one**, death reigned through **the**
> **one**, much more those who receive the abundance of grace and of
> the gift of righteousness will reign in life through **the One**, Jesus
> Christ (Rom. 5:15–17).

Did you notice the contrast between Adam and Jesus? Adam sinned and
brought death in the world. Jesus died and brought life to us.

Did you notice we are either "in Adam" or we are "in Christ?" We are
either dead in our trespasses and sins, or we are alive in Christ.

Did you notice that each man "reigned" over a kingdom? Adam's kingdom is a reign of death. Jesus reigns over a kingdom of life.

> So then as through **one transgression** there resulted **condem-**
> **nation to all men**, even so through **one act of righteousness** there
> resulted justification of **life to all men**. For as through the **one**
> **man's disobedience** the many were made sinners, even so through
> the **obedience of the One** the many will be made righteous (Rom.
> 5:18–19).

More Contrasts

> > The old man (Adam) was tested in a perfect garden by the devil
> > and failed (Gen. 3:6). The new man (Christ) was tempted in a
> > barren wilderness by the devil and succeeded (Matt. 4:10–11).
> > Jesus also passed the test of temptation in the Garden of Geth-
> > semane (Matt. 26:38–45).
> > The first Adam was made from the earth, but the Last Adam
> > (Christ) came from heaven (1 Cor. 15:47).

The Old Testament is a story of one man's failure and God's persistent effort
to rescue sinners. The New Testament is a story of one man's success in God's

persistent effort to rescue sinners. The Old Testament is about the failure of Adam while the New Testament is about the success of Jesus.

The first verse in the Old Testament reads, "In the beginning God created the heavens and the earth (Gen. 1:1). The New Testament's first words are, "In the beginning was the Word" (John 1:1).

The Old Testament begins with a man, Adam, who fails. The New Testament begins with a man, Jesus, who succeeds.

The Old Testament begins with "the book of the generations of Adam" (Gen. 5:1). The New Testament begins with "the record of the genealogy of Jesus the Messiah" (Matt. 1:1).

The Old Testament ends with the word, "curse" (Mal. 4:6). The last book of the New Testament includes the words, "no more curse" (Rev. 22:3).

The Bible is split into two testaments that tell the stories of two men. Either the authors of this fantastic story conspired to create something this amazing (highly unlikely as they lived at different times and sometimes in different countries), or the Bible is supernaturally inspired. Either the Bible is a grand lie, or it is the truth.

You Are in a Man

The world defines people by gender or skin color, but the Bible testifies there are only two types of people on the planet: those in Adam and those in Christ.

The Bible does not allow for people to be in Buddha, or in Gandhi, or in the Pope, or in Joseph Smith, or in any other religious system. You can only be in Adam or in Jesus.

Whether you know it or not, you are IN one of those two men. You are either IN Adam, the man of sin and death, or you are IN Christ, the man of grace and life.

Who are you in?

250	◉
	├ A.D. 33: Jesus crucified
	├ A.D. 30: Jesus begins ministry
	├ A.D. 26: John the Baptist begins preaching
0	◉ ├ 0: Jesus is born
	├ 397–5 B.C.: The silent years
250	◉
	├ 397 B.C.: Malachi is Israel's last prophet until John the Baptist
500	◉ ├ 515 B.C.: Jerusalem rebuilt and temple completed
	├ 536 B.C.: Jews start returning to Jerusalem
	├ 586 B.C.: Southern Kingdom falls to Babylon
750	◉ ├ 721 B.C.: Northern Kingdom falls to Assyria
	├ 975 B.C.: Israel split in two
1000	◉ ├ 1004 B.C.: Solomon's temple completed
	├ 1015 B.C.: Solomon becomes king
	├ 1055 B.C.: David becomes king
1250	◉
	├ 1451 B.C.: The Jews enter the Promised Land
	├ 1491–1451 B.C.: The Jews wander the desert
1500	◉ ├ 1491 B.C.: Moses leads the Exodus out of Egypt
	├ 1700–1574 B.C.: Joseph and his brothers have lots of babies
1750	◉ ├ 1739 B.C.: Joseph sold into slavery in Egypt
	├ 1836 B.C.: Jacob born
	├ 1896 B.C.: Isaac born
2000	◉ ├ 1996 B.C. Abraham born
2250	◉
	├ 2349 B.C.: Noah and the Global Flood
2500	◉
2750	◉
3000	◉
3250	◉
3500	◉
3750	◉
4000	◉
	├ 4004 B.C.: Creation, Adam and Eve, Cain and Abel

Timeline

4004 B.C. — A.D. 33

Jesus wants to be known as a city of refuge, not for His ability to influence the city of Washington.

Chapter 17

Jesus Is Places and Things

You have been lisped at.

John Calvin said, ". . . as nurses commonly do with infants, God is wont in measure to lisp in speaking to us."[1] How has God lisped at us? By teaching us spiritual truths with physical pictures and events.

God created places and things in the Old Testament to teach us about Jesus in the New Testament. These pictures are so simple, even a child can understand them. God graciously babbled at us so we can learn complex truths.

Nation of Israel

When Jesus was born King of the Jews, King Herod was not excited about his pint-sized competition. Herod decided the best way to deal with his tiny rival was to kill him. Nice.

---

1. John Calvin, *The Institutes*, book 1, ch.13, section 1.

An angel warned Joseph in a dream to vamoose from Israel and hightail it to Egypt and stay put until given the green light to return home.

> Now when they had gone, behold, an angel of the Lord appeared to Joseph in a dream and said, "Get up! Take the Child and His mother and **flee to Egypt**, and remain there until I tell you; for Herod is going to search for the Child to **destroy Him**."
> So Joseph got up and took the Child and His mother while it was still night, and left for **Egypt**. He remained there until the death of Herod. This was to **fulfill** what had been spoken by the Lord through the prophet: "**Out of Egypt I called My Son**" (Matt. 2:13–15).

Math

Sorry, you are going to have to do a little math. Matthew 2 tells us that Jesus was "My Son" who was "called out of Egypt" in fulfillment of a prophecy. Which prophecy?

> When **Israel** was a youth I loved him,
> And out of **Egypt** I called My **son** (Hosea 11:1).

Here comes the math: Jesus was the "son called out of Egypt." Israel was also called "out of Egypt." Therefore, Jesus equals Israel.

And you thought you would never use the transitive property of equality.[2]

Israel Is a Picture of Jesus

God promised a piece of land to Abraham in the 21st century B.C. Centuries passed and still no land was given to the Jews. Instead, the Jews were held as slaves in Egypt for centuries.

In the 15th century, a deliverer named Moses was sent by God to break the chains of bondage and bring God's chosen people into a land "flowing with milk and honey" — Canaan.

> - Both Israel and Jesus were "called out of Egypt" to the land of Israel.
> - Israel was tempted in the wilderness for 40 years and failed. Jesus was tempted in the wilderness for 40 days and succeeded.
> - Each time Jesus was tempted in the wilderness, He quoted Moses in the wilderness.

---

2. Yes, I did have to look that up.

> The Jews were brought into the Promised Land by a man named Joshua, the Hebrew name for Jesus. We are brought into the heavenly promised land by Jesus.
> The story of the Jews being delivered from Egypt and brought to the Promised Land is a picture of the redemptive work of Jesus. Just as the Jews were delivered out of slavery to Pharaoh by Moses, we are delivered out of slavery to Satan by Jesus.

Canaan was a land of giant cities and giant men (Num. 14:28). How could an unarmed, untrained, undisciplined people possibly remove such a formidable force and enter this "heaven"? They couldn't. God had to bring them to paradise.

> Be strong and courageous, do not be afraid or tremble at them, for the LORD your God **is the one who goes with you**. He will not fail you or forsake you (Deut. 31:6).

The story of Israel is a picture of Jesus and the gospel. The Jews could not enter the Promised Land without God's help and we can't enter heaven unless God provides a way. But Israel was not the only place that is a picture of Jesus and His redemptive work.

City of Refuge

> Then the LORD spoke to Moses, saying, "Speak to the sons of Israel and say to them, 'When you cross the Jordan into the land of Canaan, then you shall select for yourselves cities to be your **cities of refuge**, that the manslayer who has killed any person unintentionally may flee there.
>
> The cities shall be to you **as a refuge from the avenger**, so that the manslayer will **not die** until he stands before the congregation for trial. The cities which you are to give shall be your six **cities of refuge**.
>
> You shall give three cities across the Jordan and three cities in the land of Canaan; they are to be **cities of refuge**. These six cities shall be for refuge for the sons of Israel, and for the alien and for the sojourner among them; that anyone who kills a person unintentionally may **flee there** (Num. 35:9–14).

What a kind thing for God do to. Living in the 15th century B.C. was a rather scary time to live. Even though God gave laws and a court system with judges (but no lawyers!), men would frequently act as vigilantes and take justice into their own hands. To ensure that a man who ACCIDENTALLY killed another man did not go swimming with the fishes, God created six cities of refuge.

The suspected criminal was to run to the nearest city of refuge and lay his hands on a special altar. He was safe there. The pursuing angry mob could not touch him until a trial could be held to determine innocence or guilt (Num. 35:6–34).

We can learn much from this concept.

We Do Not Shoot Abortion Doctors

Yes, abortion doctors are murderers. Yes, they are right near the bottom of the immorality barrel, but we are not to take matters of justice into our own hands and kill them.

The city of refuge tells us that God wants judges to determine the innocence or guilt of a suspected criminal. It is not up to a citizen to execute justice. As horrible as abortion is, we cannot shoot an abortion doctor. That is not our role.

Realms of Authority

Just as in the Old Testament, God has set up realms of authority in the New Testament. There are three:

1. Family: two parents have very great authority over a few.
2. Church: shepherds have some authority over many.
3. Government: authorities have very little authority over everyone.

Notice, the smaller the number of people, the greater the authority; the greater number of people, the less authority.

Each one of these realms has very specific assignments.

1. Parents are to train up their children in the discipline and admonition of the Lord (Eph. 6:1).
2. Shepherds are to feed the flock and protect them from wolves (Eph. 4:11).
3. Government officials are to punish bad guys (Rom. 13:1–7).

Coloring Within the Lines

Any time one of the realms of authority gets involved in one of the other realms, disaster follows. The reason big government programs like welfare or Obamacare cannot and will not work is because taking care of the poor and sick is not the job of the government.

Big government is not a bad idea because it fails. Big government fails because it is not biblical.

That rule also applies to the Church. Any time the Church gets involved with government affairs, bad results will ensue. Why? Because the Church is not the state. God, not Thomas Jefferson, is the One who created the correct definition of "separation of Church and state."

Yes, Christians can work for the government.

Yes, Christians can and should vote.

Yes, the Church can preach to the government and tell them to behave biblically.

But that is as far as it should go if we are going to color within the lines that God has drawn for us.

As soon as unbelievers start seeing Christians as a political party and not as followers of Jesus Christ, we have stepped over the line.

As soon as unbelievers hate us because of the way we vote, then we have acted more like a political party than Christians.

The world will hate Christians (John 15:18), but the world should hate us because we are followers of the Lord Jesus Christ, not because we are Republicans.

Christians are not called to be the Moral Majority; we are called to make disciples (Matt. 28:19–20). Imposing morality is what the Pharisees did, and Jesus did not take too kindly to them. Unbelievers can't even be moral without Jesus. To impose morality on unbelievers is like asking a dog to do algebra.

The message of Jesus is not "Be good." The Christian gospel is "You are not good. You need a Savior who is good." The Christian gospel is not "Vote this way." Does that mean we do not participate in the marketplace of ideas or the political arena? Nope. It just means that our predominant message must be the Gospel, not morality.

Jesus wants to be known as a city of refuge, not for His ability to influence the city of Washington.

The Best Lesson

In the same way God, desiring even more to show to the heirs of the promise the unchangeableness of His purpose, interposed with an oath, so that by two unchangeable things in which it is impossible for God to lie, we who have **taken refuge** would have strong encouragement to **take hold** of the hope set before us. This hope we have as an anchor of the soul, a hope both sure and steadfast and one which enters within the **veil**, where Jesus has entered as a forerunner for us, having become a **high priest** forever according to the order of Melchizedek (Heb. 6:17–20).

Jesus Is a Much Better City of Refuge

> Innocent men were to run to the city of refuge. We are not innocent; we are actually guilty.
> The city of refuge was temporary; Jesus is permanent.
> The city of refuge is a thing. Jesus is an actual person with whom we can have a relationship.

God may have been lisping when He gave the Jews cities of refuge, but the lesson is crystal clear in Jesus.

Jacob's Ladder

He (Jacob) had a dream, and behold, a **ladder** was set on the earth with its top **reaching to heaven**; and behold, the angels of God were **ascending** and **descending** on it (Gen. 28:12).

Either Jacob had too much mutton for dinner, or his dream was actually a picture of the Lamb of God. Jesus said to Nathanael, "Truly, truly, I say to you, you will see the heavens opened and the angels of God **ascending and descending on the Son of Man**" (John 1:51).

In Jacob's dream, an actual ladder came down from heaven so angels could go up and down from heaven to earth. Jesus was telling Nathanael that He was Jacob's ladder, only better.

Jesus, like the ladder, came down from heaven, but instead of providing a way for angels to get from heaven to earth, Jesus provides a way for man to get from earth to heaven.

Remember, Jesus is the ladder who brings us up to heaven. We do not climb our way to heaven, Jesus brings us there. We are not army recruits who can climb to the top rung. We are dead men who need to be carried completely by Jesus.

Jesus Is Our Surety

In legal terms, a surety is one who promises to pay the debt if the principal cannot or will not pay his debt. In the Old Testament we see many examples of this: Genesis 43:9, 44:32–34; Psalm 119:122; and Proverbs 6:1.

Jesus is the guarantee (surety) of a better covenant (Heb. 7:22).

> We have more than a financial debt, we have a sin debt.
> Our debt is not with man, but God.
> Jesus does more than pay our fine, He puts righteousness into our account.
> Jesus continues to pay our fine, day after day after day.

God will never un-forgive you. He will never regret accepting you. God will always love you with the same love that He has for His very own Son. Why? Because His very own Son is the surety of the new covenant.

Never, ever worry that God will change His mind about you. He can't. If you are in Christ, you will forever be loved by the Father because of the work of the Son.

Your Debt

Perhaps you have been trying to climb your way to heaven on the ladder of your own works. Perhaps you have been taught that is what you must do in order to inherit eternal life. Jesus makes it clear, only He can pay your debt and only He can bring you to heaven.

Your efforts don't even get you to the first rung of the ladder. In fact, your efforts to save yourself only increase your sin debt. God hates self-effort. He has given His only Son to be the surety for you. He is willing to pay your debt, but you must lay down your efforts and trust in Him.

Rest on Jesus. He has done it all. He will do it all. Let Him pay your fine with the Father and bring you safely home.

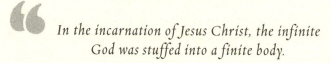

In the incarnation of Jesus Christ, the infinite God was stuffed into a finite body.

A CRUTCH

Chapter 18

Jesus Is the New Covenant, Part One

There are two types of people who take vacations:

> People who take historic bus tours.
> People who mock people who take historic bus tours. Especially duck tours.

While you do indeed lose your dignity on a double-decker bus with a perky tour guide, you definitely learn a lot. For instance, if you took a bus tour through the historic and humid city of Savannah, you would learn that the founders of this mossy city wanted to outlaw three things.

1. Alcohol. Baptists would have flocked to Savannah if that had passed.
2. Roman Catholics. Baptists would probably love that too. The founders of Savannah were Protestants who well remembered

the treatment they received in Europe under Roman Catholic monarchs like bloody Queen Mary.

3. Lawyers. Everyone would love that. The founders knew that clever lawyers could make a hash out of what was plain and turn something simple into complete confusion.

Thanks to many (not all) modern-day lawyers, legal contracts are a dime a dozen. Scratch that — they are $250 per hour a dozen, but if you can afford a more expensive lawyer than the lawyer who drew up the contract, you can get yourself out of just about any modern-day contract.

Not So With Covenants

In Bible days, a covenant (another word for "contract") was a "till death do us part" kind of affair. Actually, it was more than that — covenants were an "if I break this, you can kill me" kind of contract. Needless to say, a man did not enter into a covenant lightly.

A covenant was a two-way commitment unto death with a willingness to die or be killed in defending one's covenant partner. There isn't a lawyer on the planet who would draw up a contract like that today.

A Big Deal

The Mosaic covenant was cut between God and man in the 14th century B.C. For the next eight centuries, the Mosaic covenant was the law of the land.

Suddenly, a prophet named Jeremiah made a major announcement: God is going to cut a new covenant. As there had only been a few biblical covenants in the history of the world, this was a very, very big deal.

> "Behold, days are **coming**," declares the LORD, "when I will make a **new covenant** with the house of Israel and with the house of Judah, **not like the covenant** which I made with their fathers in the day I took them by the hand to bring them out of the land of Egypt, My covenant which **they broke,** although I was a husband to them," declares the LORD. "But this is the covenant which I will make with the house of Israel after those days," declares the LORD, "I will put My **law within them** and on their heart I will write it; and I will be their God, and they shall be My people. They will not teach again, each man his neighbor and each man his brother, saying, 'Know the LORD,' for they will all know Me, from the least of them to the greatest of them," declares the LORD, "for **I will forgive their iniquity**, and their **sin I will remember no more**" (Jer. 31:31–34).

It is safe to say that millions of gallons of blood had been shed for the covering of sins during the eight centuries the Jews labored under the Mosaic covenant.

Lamb after lamb. Blood upon blood with no relief from their guilty conscience.

The prophet Jeremiah proclaimed the best news an observant Jew could ever hear: a new covenant is coming that will forgive your sins! That was beyond good news, that was magnificent news.

Then Silence

Jeremiah announced a new covenant was going to be cut by God Himself, but six centuries went by and no more news from God about this wonderful new covenant. In fact, there was complete silence after Malachi wrote the last book of the Old Testament in the late fifth century B.C. Not a single prophet appeared to bring any news to the Jews. Nothing. Where was God? When will this new covenant be cut?

John the Baptist

The words of John the Baptist broke centuries of prophetic silence when he pointed at Jesus and announced, "Behold the lamb of God, who **takes away the sin** of the world" (John 1:29).

Finally, a prophet proclaiming that the new covenant had arrived. Finally.

But how? How would this covenant be cut? What would be the promises of this new covenant?

Ten Steps to Cutting Covenant

Here are two biblical examples of a covenant-cutting ceremony.

> Then Jonathan **made a covenant** with David because he loved him as himself. Jonathan stripped himself of the **robe** that was on him and **gave it** to David, with his **armor**, including his **sword** and his **bow** and his **belt** (1 Sam. 18:3–4).

God Himself went through a covenant-cutting ceremony when He entered into covenant with Abraham.

> So He [God] said to him [Abraham], "Bring Me a three year old **heifer**, and a three year old female **goat**, and a three year old **ram**, and a turtledove, and a young pigeon." Then he brought all these to Him and **cut them in two**, and laid each half opposite the other;

but he did not cut the birds. The birds of prey came down upon the carcasses, and Abram drove them away.

Now when the sun was going down, a **deep sleep** fell upon Abram; and behold, terror and great darkness fell upon him. . . .

It came about when the sun had set, that it was very dark, and behold, there appeared a **smoking oven** and a **flaming torch** which **passed between** these pieces (Gen. 15:9–17).

Today a piece of paper is signed to enter into a contract; biblical covenants were elaborate procedures with dramatic symbolism. Here is some of the symbolism in the Abrahamic covenant.

> Animals were cut in two (Gen. 15:9–10).
> Abraham slept while God cut the covenant, signifying that God alone made this agreement (Gen. 15:12). The Abrahamic covenant is God's forever promise to the Jews.
> The smoking oven and flaming torch symbolically represented God.
> The oven and torch alone passed between the sacrificed animals while God made an oath to provide a land, nation, and seed.
> The dead animals symbolized the consequences of breaking one's covenant oath.

Please remember, a covenant is typically a two-way street; both partners have responsibilities in a covenant with one another. Jesus initiated the new covenant, brings us into the new covenant, keeps us in the new covenant, and helps us obey the new covenant. But we have to act in response to His covenantal work.

We are brought into the new covenant of grace entirely by the work of Jesus. We are kept in the new covenant entirely by Jesus. But we are given terms that we are to follow in response to all that He has done, which is everything.

In light of how ancient covenants were cut, let's take a look at the new covenant. How exactly did Jesus cut this covenant for us?

Step #1: An Exchange of Robes or Outer Garments

Today, we have closets full of clothes; that was hardly the case in biblical times. When someone in the Old Testament would say, "I simply don't have a thing to wear," they probably meant it.

One's robe was their garment. Of course, there were garments worn underneath the robe, but the robe was used so often the person was actually known by his robe. You would only have to see the back of someone's robe to know who was wearing it. In essence, you were your robe and your robe was you. It was your identity.

Furthermore, the robe was not just an outer garment, it served as a blanket or pillow. The robe was precious to a person. The robe was the person.

In covenant, two become one. The exchange of robes was an outward sign of an inward commitment. By making this exchange, covenant partners were saying that they were receiving that person unto themselves. It was a total exchange of identity.

Did Jesus Take on Our Identity?

> Have this attitude in yourselves which was also in Christ Jesus, who, although He existed in the form of God, did not regard equality with God a thing to be grasped, but emptied Himself, **taking the form** of a bond-servant, and being **made in the likeness of men**. Being found in **appearance as a man**, He humbled Himself by becoming obedient to the point of death, even death on a cross (Phil. 2:5–8).

The King of Glory left His throne, humbled Himself and took on our actual form. God became flesh and became one of us.

The Greatest Miracle Ever

If you had to pick the greatest miracle of all time, which miracle would you choose?

1. The creation of the universe
2. The incarnation
3. The popularity of Honey Boo Boo

While the answer might seem obvious, the greatest miracle ever is not the success of Honey Boo Boo. The greatest miracle ever is not the creation of everything that exists. The greatest miracle of all time is the incarnation of Jesus Christ.

In the incarnation of Jesus Christ, the infinite God was stuffed into a finite body. The all-powerful, omni-present second member of the Trinity miraculously became man.

Muslims are wrongly taught that God was intimate with Mary. The Bible teaches that Mary, the sinner, was "overshadowed by the Holy Spirit" (Luke 1:35). God supernaturally made Mary pregnant without conjugal relations. That is why Jesus is fully God and fully man. This is the hypostatic union of Jesus Christ, the God-man.

If Jesus had had two earthly parents, He would have been born a sinner. If Jesus had been born through a sexual union between God and a human, Jesus would have been born a sinner. Because Jesus is not of Adam's seed, He was not born in sin and He did not inherit a sin nature.

Instead, God the Holy Spirit overshadowed Mary, and Jesus was miraculously conceived without sin. Roman Catholics like to teach that Mary was perfect and that she herself was immaculately conceived. This is wrong for many reasons.

1. It is not necessary. Because the Holy Spirit "overshadowed" her, Jesus did not inherit sinful DNA from an earthly father.
2. The Bible says that there is not a single human on the planet who was or is perfect. Only the God-man Jesus Christ has fulfilled that description.
3. Mary herself knew she was a sinner who needed saving when she called God her "Savior" (Luke 1:47).

Ontological Nature of Jesus Christ

Jesus is 100 percent God and 100 percent man. His two natures are neither mingled nor confused. Jesus was not a superman. Jesus was not a demi-god. Jesus was and is the unique, only begotten (one of a kind) Son of God (John 3:16).

Early Church councils debated the issue of Jesus' ontological nature (how He is "put together") in extreme detail. The Athanasian Creed was penned after years of intense debate over Christology (the study of Jesus). In the early Church, the debate was rarely about the divinity of Jesus; that was broadly accepted. The debate surrounded His human nature. How could the infinite God become finite flesh?

The early Church took painstaking effort to make sure their Christology was correct. They took these warnings seriously:

> Who is the liar but the one who denies that Jesus is the Christ? This is the antichrist, the one who denies the Father and the Son (1 John 2:22).

> For many deceivers have gone out into the world, those who do not acknowledge Jesus Christ as coming in the flesh. This is the deceiver and the antichrist (2 John 7).

Understanding Jesus rightly is so important that the authors of the Athanasian Creed labored long and hard to clarify Christology (theology about Jesus). Please note, if you don't understand the nature of Jesus rightly, you don't understand God rightly because Jesus Himself is God.

Athanasian Creed

Whosoever will be saved, before all things it is necessary that he hold the catholic [this is not the Roman Catholic Church, but a small *c* catholic which means "universal"] faith. Which faith **except everyone do keep** whole and undefiled, without doubt he shall **perish everlastingly**. And the catholic faith is this: That we worship one God in Trinity, and Trinity in Unity, neither confounding the persons, nor dividing the substance.

For there is **one** Person of the Father, **another** of the Son, and **another** of the Holy Spirit. But the godhead of the Father, of the Son, and of the Holy Spirit, **is all one**, the glory equal, the majesty co-eternal.

Such as the Father is, such is the Son, and such is the Holy Spirit. The Father uncreated, the Son uncreated, and the Holy Spirit uncreated. The Father incomprehensible, the Son incomprehensible, and the Holy Spirit incomprehensible.

The Father eternal, the Son eternal, and the Holy Spirit eternal. And yet they are **not three eternals, but one Eternal**.

As also there are not three incomprehensibles, nor three uncreated, but one Uncreated, and one Incomprehensible. So likewise the Father is Almighty, the Son Almighty, and the Holy Spirit Almighty. And yet they are **not three almighties, but one Almighty**.

So the Father is God, the Son is God, and the Holy Spirit is God. And yet they are not three gods, but **one God**.

So likewise the Father is Lord, the Son Lord, and the Holy Spirit Lord. And yet **not three lords, but one Lord**.

For as we are compelled by the Christian verity to acknowledge each Person by Himself to be both God and Lord, so we are also **forbidden** by the catholic religion to say that there are three gods or three lords.

The Father is made of none, neither created, nor begotten. The Son is of the Father alone, not made, nor created, but begotten. The Holy Spirit is of the Father, neither made, nor created, nor begotten, but proceeding.

So there is one Father, not three fathers; one Son, not three sons; one Holy Spirit, not three holy spirits.

And in the Trinity **none is before or after another**; none is greater or less than another, but all three Persons are co-eternal together and co-equal. So that in all things, as is aforesaid, the Unity in Trinity and the Trinity in Unity is to be worshipped.

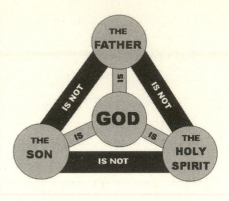

He therefore that will be saved must think thus of the Trinity.

Whew! That was a lot of theology, and that is only half of the Creed. The first half of the creed focused on the doctrine of the Trinity. The Athanasian Creed makes it clear, if we don't understand the Trinity rightly, we will not be saved.

Athanasian Creed, Cont'd.

Furthermore, it is **necessary to everlasting salvation** that he also believe **rightly the Incarnation** of our Lord Jesus Christ. For the right faith is, that we believe and confess, that our Lord Jesus Christ, the Son of God, is **God and man**; God, of the substance of the Father, begotten before the worlds; and man **of the substance of his mother**, born in the world; **perfect God and perfect man**, of a rational soul and human flesh subsisting.

Equal to the Father, as touching His godhead; and inferior to the Father, as touching His manhood; who, although He is God and man, yet **he is not two, but one Christ**; one, not by conversion of the godhead into flesh but by taking of the manhood into God; one altogether; **not by confusion** of substance, but by **unity** of person.

This is the catholic [universal] faith, which except a man believe faithfully, he cannot be saved.

That is how important correct theology is; or at least used to be. Either those old dead guys had it right, or pastors who enter their Sunday service on horses are right. It's probably wise to stick with the Bible and the serious saints of old.

Jesus Took on More Than Our Flesh

He made Him who knew no sin **to be sin** on our behalf, so that we might become the righteousness of God in Him (2 Cor. 5:21).

Our sin was placed on Him and His righteousness is placed on us. Jesus received our sin and we receive His righteousness. Talk about a lopsided exchange!

Martin Luther once said, "Jesus, you are my righteousness. I am your sin."

Do We "Put On" Jesus?

Remember, covenant is a two-way street. Jesus put on our nature and took on our sin. While we do nothing to earn credit for the salvation He provides, there are still terms for us in the covenant. Just as He took on our nature, we are to take on His.

> But **put on the Lord Jesus Christ,** and make no provision for the flesh in regard to its lusts (Rom. 13:14).

> For all of you who were baptized into Christ have **clothed yourselves with Christ** (Gal. 3:27).

The exchange of robes was an outward sign of an inward commitment. In making this exchange, covenant partners were saying that they were receiving that person unto themselves. It was a total exchange of identity; that is why we are called to be "imitators of Christ" (1 Cor. 11:1; Eph. 5:1).

When God grants us repentance and faith in Jesus Christ, we enter into the new covenant of grace, merging ourselves into Him.

> Therefore if you have been raised up with Christ, keep seeking the things above, where Christ is, seated at the right hand of God. Set your mind on the things above, not on the things that are on earth. For you have died and **your life is hidden with Christ in God**. When Christ, who is our life, is revealed, then you also will be revealed with Him in glory.

> Therefore consider the members of your earthly body as **dead to immorality, impurity, passion, evil desire, and greed**, which amounts to idolatry. For it is because of these things that the wrath of God will come upon the sons of disobedience, and in them you also once walked, when you were living in them.

> But now you also, **put them all aside**: anger, wrath, malice, slander, and abusive speech from your mouth. Do not lie to one another, since you laid aside the **old self** with its evil practices, and have **put on the new self** who is being renewed to a true knowledge **according to the image of the One** who created him — a renewal in which there is no distinction between Greek and Jew, circumcised

and uncircumcised, barbarian, Scythian, slave and freeman, but Christ is all, and in all.

So, as those who have been chosen of God, holy and beloved, **put on** a heart of compassion, kindness, humility, gentleness and patience; bearing with one another, and forgiving each other, whoever has a complaint against anyone; just as the Lord forgave you, so also should you. Beyond all these things **put on** love, which is the perfect bond of unity (Col. 3:1–14).

The Great Exchange

Jesus took your sin upon Himself and died for you. In exchange for that great gift, we are to die to our old selves, our old loves, our old sins.

I have been **crucified with Christ**; and it is no longer I who live, but Christ lives in me; and the life which I now live in the flesh I live by faith in the Son of God, who loved me and gave Himself up for me (Gal. 2:20).

Therefore **be imitators** of God, as beloved children; and walk in love, **just as** Christ also loved you and gave Himself up for us, an offering and a sacrifice to God as a fragrant aroma (Eph. 5:1–2).

Step #2: The Exchange of Weapons

When Jonathan and David exchanged weapons, these covenant partners symbolized their responsibility to defend each other against their enemies. In doing this, they were saying, "My weapons are at your disposal. I will lay down my life to protect you." Jonathan was obligated to defend David's life, even if it meant going against his own father.

God Defends Us

This is a plain indication of God's righteous judgment so that you will be considered worthy of the kingdom of God, for which indeed **you are suffering**. For after all it is only just for **God to repay** with affliction those who afflict you, and to give relief to **you who are afflicted** and to us as well when the Lord Jesus will be revealed from heaven with His mighty angels in flaming fire (2 Thess. 1:5–7).

If God defends His children (and He does), how are we to treat those who hurt us?

Never pay back evil for evil to anyone. Respect what is right in the sight of all men. If possible, so far as it depends on you, be at peace with all men. **Never take your own revenge**, beloved, but leave room for the wrath of God for it is written, "**Vengeance is mine, I will repay**," says the Lord (Rom. 12:17–19).

The next time someone hurts you, remember, you have a covenant partner who will defend you. You do not have to retaliate; God will ensure that justice is satisfied.

The Hardest Math

Russell D. Moore says that the hardest math in the world is 70 times 7.

Then Peter came and said to Him, "Lord, how often shall my brother sin against me and I forgive him? Up to seven times?" Jesus said to him, "I do not say to you, up to seven times, but up to seventy times seven (Matt. 18:21–22).

Jesus was not doing forgiveness math when He commanded us to forgive 490 times. He was telling us to forgive as we have been forgiven (Eph. 4:31). That is a lot.

How Can We Do That?

We know that we have been forgiven so much, how can we withhold forgiveness from anyone?

God will make sure that person's sin is dealt with. Either that person will be punished in hell for their sin, or Jesus will have been punished on their behalf IF that person is in Christ or becomes a Christian.

Even Harder

"But if your enemy is hungry, feed him, and if he is thirsty, give him a drink; for in so doing you will heap burning coals on his head." Do not be overcome by evil, but overcome evil with good (Rom. 12:20–21).

We have a covenant partner who will deal with retribution one way or another. This frees you to "love your neighbor as yourself" (Mark 12:31), even when that person sins against you.

Does this mean you have to expose yourself to evil and stay in a wicked, abusive relationship? Certainly not. But it does mean that you should forgive and always live in hope of potential reconciliation IF the person is no longer abusive.

Jesus modeled this attitude for us spectacularly on the Cross. He had just been physically abused, taunted, mocked, humiliated, shamed, spat upon, beaten, and whipped when he prayed to God, "Father, forgive them; for they do not know what they are doing" (Luke 23:34).

Jesus said that, even as He was being punished for their sins against Him. Is it hard to forgive? Yes. But we have a role model and we have a motivation: Jesus has forgiven us for far more than anything anyone has ever done to us.

Constantly remember, "We all carry Jesus' nails in our pockets."

> Yes, people have hurt you. And you killed Jesus.
> Yes, people have slandered you. And you killed Jesus.
> Yes, people have disappointed you. And you killed Jesus.
> Yes, people have stolen from you. And you killed Jesus.
> Yes, people cut you off in traffic. And you killed Jesus.
> Yes, your friend gossiped about you. And you killed Jesus.
> Yes, your parents ignored you. And you killed Jesus.
> Yes, your kids are frustrating. And you killed Jesus.
> Yes, your neighbor neglects his yard. And you killed Jesus.

Forgive, knowing that you have been forgiven much. Forgive, knowing that you have a covenant partner who is defending you.

Are We Supposed to Defend God?

Covenant is a two-way street. God defends us — are we supposed to defend God?

God hardly needs our help, yet we are called to defend His Word.

Beloved, while I was making every effort to write you about our common salvation, I felt the necessity to write to you appealing that you **contend earnestly** for the faith which was once for all handed down to the **saints** (Jude 3).

As God's saints, we are commanded to defend His Word. After all, His Word is:

> Ordained by God Himself (Ps. 119:4)
> The way to remain pure (Ps. 119:9)
> Filled with wonderful things (Ps. 119:18)

> A great counselor (Ps. 119:24)
> A great strengthener (Ps. 119:28)
> The way to not be vain (Ps. 119:37)
> The way to salvation (Ps. 119:41)
> The way of liberty (Ps. 119:45)
> The path of goodness (Ps. 119:68)
> Better than thousands of gold and silver pieces (Ps. 119:72)
> The way to not feel guilty (Ps. 119:80)
> Settled in heaven (Ps. 119:89)
> A delight (Ps. 119:92)
> A reviver (Ps. 119:93)
> The way to become wise (Ps. 119:98)
> Sweeter than honey (Ps. 119:103)
> A lamp to your feet and a light to your path (Ps. 119:105)
> A joy to your heart (Ps. 119:111)
> A sustainer (Ps. 119:116)
> Above fine gold (Ps. 119:127)
> Wonderful (Ps. 119:129)
> Very pure (Ps. 119:140)
> Righteous (Ps. 119:144)
> Truth (Ps. 119:151)
> Founded forever (Ps. 119:152)
> Salvation (Ps. 119:155)
> Great treasure (Ps. 119:162)

God's Word so closely resembles God Himself, when we defend God's Word, we are indeed defending God. And these days, God's Word needs lots of defending.

Not Siding with God's Enemies

When we side with false teachers, we are siding with God's enemies.

More than that, every time we partner with the world, we are partnering with God's enemies and thereby, siding against God.

You **adulteresses**, do you not know that friendship **with the world** is **hostility** toward God? Therefore whoever wishes to be a friend of the world makes himself **an enemy of God** (James 4:4).

Whoa. Did you catch that? When you sin by siding with the world system, you are an adulterer. When you sin, you are "having an affair" with the world and cheating on your covenant partner. Ponder that the next time you are tempted.

Are You an Adulterer?

How might you be doing that? What do you covet? What trifle do you think you need to have? What are the things on your "bucket list"? By loving the things of this world, you are showing disdain for your God.

What is your pet sin? What is the vice you struggle to give up? When you continue to "make love" to your sin, you are committing spiritual adultery against your Savior.

> Or do you think that the Scripture speaks to no purpose: "He
> **jealously desires** the Spirit which He has made to dwell in us"? But
> He gives a greater grace. Therefore it says, "God is opposed to the
> proud, but gives grace to the humble" (James 4:5–6).

God, your covenant partner, is jealous for you. Yes, the Bible says that jealousy is a sin (Gal. 5:26), but this type of jealousy is an appropriate form of jealousy. Are you not jealous for the faithfulness and affection of your spouse? Yes, and you are not sinning. The same thing is true with God.

Sinful jealousy is desiring something that doesn't belong to you, but you belong to God and He jealously desires you. After all, He gives us everything, is it too much of Him to ask us for everything in return?

Step #3: The Exchange of Belts or Girdles

The belt of the garment held one's weapons in place. It was a symbol of a man's strength. To give another your belt in covenant signified the giving of your strength to your covenant partner.

Does God give us strength to endure persecution? Paul said, "I can do all things through Him who strengthens me" (Phil. 4:13).

This verse is not intended to mean that a Christian can do everything he sets his mind to. Evander Holyfield displayed this verse on his boxing trunks when he got knocked out by Mike Tyson. Plenty of Christians who have taken Philippians 4:13 as their life verse filed for bankruptcy.

This verse tells us that God will help us endure all hardship when we are persecuted for our service to Him. Our covenant partner gives us the strength to endure.

Do We Give God Our Strength?

Ha! We have no strength. All we give to God is our weaknesses. Once again, we get the much better end of the bargain.

> And He has said to me, "My grace is **sufficient** for you, for power is perfected in **weakness**." Most gladly, therefore, I will rather boast about **my weaknesses**, so that the **power of Christ** may dwell in me. Therefore I am well content with **weaknesses**, with insults, with distresses, with persecutions, with difficulties, for Christ's sake; for when I am **weak**, then I am **strong** (2 Cor. 12:9–10).

We get His righteousness and He gets our sins. We give Him our weaknesses and He gives us His strength. Anyone with an ounce of sense would advise, "You would have to be a fool to not enter into this covenant."

Step #4: The Cutting of Wrists Signifying Oneness

When you and I make an agreement, we sign our names with ink and shake each other's hands. Biblical covenant was far more serious and symbolic.

When a covenant was cut, the two parties would strike hands. Frequently an incision would be made and wrists were locked in such a way so their blood would mix with one other. This co-mingling signified that they had become "blood brothers." In essence, two had become one.

In keeping with the oneness of blood brothers, consider Colossians 1:27, and note how it shows the oneness that is ours with Jesus Christ.

> To whom God willed to make known what is the riches of the glory of this mystery among the Gentiles, which is **Christ in you**, the hope of glory.

If you are a Christian, Christ is dwelling in you with the power of His Holy Spirit (Rom. 8:9–11; Eph. 3:17) and you are in Christ (Rom. 8:1; 1 Cor. 15:22).

It is the blood of Jesus that was shed that we might be made His brother (Matt. 12:49–50).

Step #5: The Taking of an Oath

Typically, while the hands were struck an oath would be taken. The two participants would speak an oath of curses and blessings of the covenant. In doing this, they would list all of their resources that would now be made available to their new covenant partner, basically saying, "All that I have is now yours."

A witness would record this in a testament of the covenant. Deuteronomy 28 is a good example of this.

Does God Share His Possessions with Us?

And my God will **supply all your needs** according to His riches in glory in Christ Jesus (Phil. 4:19).

He who did not spare His own Son, but delivered Him over for us all, how will He not also with Him freely **give us all things**? (Rom. 8:32).

Are We to Share Our Possessions with God?

Therefore I urge you, brethren, by the mercies of God, to **present your bodies** a living and holy sacrifice, acceptable to God, which is your spiritual service of worship (Rom. 12:1).

Or do you not know that your body is a temple of the Holy Spirit who is in you, whom you have from God, and that **you are not your own**? For you have been bought with a price: therefore glorify God **in your body** (1 Cor. 6:19–20).

We might say we are willing to die for God, but are we willing to live for Him? Should we not happily live for the One who temporarily gave up His throne for our sakes?

God performed the greatest miracle of all time — He became flesh for you. He lived for you. He died for you. Are you dying to yourself, living for Him?

250	●
	┤ A.D. 33: Jesus crucified
	┤ A.D. 30: Jesus begins ministry
	┤ A.D. 26: John the Baptist begins preaching
0	◉ ┤ 0: Jesus is born
	┤ 397–5 B.C.: The silent years
250	◉
	┤ 397 B.C.: Malachi is Israel's last prophet until John the Baptist
500	◉ ┤ 515 B.C.: Jerusalem rebuilt and temple completed
	┤ 536 B.C.: Jews start returning to Jerusalem
	┤ 586 B.C.: Southern Kingdom falls to Babylon
750	◉ ┤ 721 B.C.: Northern Kingdom falls to Assyria
	┤ 975 B.C.: Israel split in two
1000	◉ ┤ 1004 B.C.: Solomon's temple completed
	┤ 1015 B.C.: Solomon becomes king
	┤ 1055 B.C.: David becomes king
1250	◉
	┤ 1451 B.C.: The Jews enter the Promised Land
	┤ 1491–1451 B.C.: The Jews wander the desert
1500	◉ ┤ 1491 B.C.: Moses leads the Exodus out of Egypt
	┤ 1700–1574 B.C.: Joseph and his brothers have lots of babies
1750	◉ ┤ 1739 B.C.: Joseph sold into slavery in Egypt
	┤ 1836 B.C.: Jacob born
	┤ 1896 B.C.: Isaac born
2000	◉ ┤ 1996 B.C. Abraham born
2250	◉
	┤ 2349 B.C.: Noah and the Global Flood
2500	◉
2750	◉
3000	◉
3250	◉
3500	◉
3750	◉
4000	◉
	┤ 4004 B.C.: Creation, Adam and Eve, Cain and Abel

Timeline
4004 B.C. – A.D. 33

Being persecuted is a sign of being a Christian.

Chapter 19

Jesus Is the New Covenant, Part Two

Sequels are rarely as good as the originals. Case in point:

> *Rocky Balboa*
> *Honey, I Blew Up the Kid*
> Any movie with a number behind it.

Let's hope this chapter does not flop like *Arthur II*.

This is the second half of the ten steps to cutting a covenant. According to several critics we consulted, this chapter is more like *The Empire Strikes Back* than *Teenage Mutant Ninja Turtles IV*. (Yes, they made four. Four!)

Step #6: Seal of the Covenant

What is your wedding ring? Among other things, it is a reminder of the covenant you entered when you vowed to be faithful to your spouse — "till death do you part." Your wedding ring is a seal of your covenant promise.

Biblical covenants regularly had signs or seals to remind the covenant partners of their promise and obligations. After the taking of the oath and the cutting of wrists, the covenant partners would take sand or dirt and rub it deep in the wound so that a scar would develop. The seal was a visible reminder of their promise given to their covenant partner.

> The seal of the Noahic covenant was the rainbow (Gen. 9:13).
> The Abrahamic covenant seal was circumcision (Gen. 17:9–14).
> The seal of the Mosaic covenant was the Sabbath (Exod. 31:13–17).

New Covenant Seal

God's seal in the new covenant is the Holy Spirit.

> In Him, you also, after listening to the message of truth, the gospel of your salvation — having also believed, you were **sealed in Him** with the **Holy Spirit** of promise, (Eph. 1:13).

Our outward "seal of the covenant" with the new covenant is to walk in the newness of life, bearing fruit in keeping with repentance (Luke 3:8).

Do we bear any physical seals on our bodies? Perhaps Paul had this in mind when he wrote:

> From now on let no one cause trouble for me, for I **bear on my body** the brand-marks of Jesus (Gal. 6:17).

Being persecuted is a sign of being a Christian.

> Indeed, all who desire to live godly in Christ Jesus will be persecuted (1 Tim. 3:12).

Step #7: The Exchange of Names

Covenant partners would exchange names upon entering the contract. Historically, that is why women would take the name of her covenant partner: to indicate an exchange of identity.

When God cut the Abrahamic covenant, Abram became Abraham. Sarai became Sarah. God became the God of Abraham (Gen. 17:5, 8, 15).

When you repent and trust Jesus, God's name changes to the God of (insert your name here).

What about us? When we become Christians, do we get a new name? Yes, we become children of God.

Our Old Names

And you were **dead in your trespasses** and sins, in which you formerly walked according to the course of this world, according to the **prince of the power of the air**, of the spirit that is now working in the sons of disobedience. Among them we too all formerly lived in the lusts of our flesh, indulging the desires of the flesh and of the mind, and were by nature **children of wrath**, even as the rest (Eph. 2:1–3).

Before God saved you:

> You were dead (Eph. 2:1). Now you are alive (Eph. 2:5).
> You were under the power of the devil (Eph. 2:2). Now you are under the power of the Holy Spirit (Gal. 5:25).
> You were a child of wrath (Eph. 2:3). Now you are a child of God (2 Cor. 6:18).

You were formerly child of Satan, now you are Child of God. But did you know that God has a special name reserved for you?

Your New, New Name

To him who overcomes . . . I will give him a white stone, and a **new name** written on the stone which no one knows but he who receives it (Rev. 2:17).

Your new name will astound you when you receive it because that name will accurately describe the essence of who you are. It will nail you to a t.

Don't even try to figure out what your new, special name will be; you can't figure it out. Your special name will be given from the One who knows you better than you know yourself.

How deeply does God know you? When you receive your new name, you will realize that there is One who knows you intimately, profoundly, and lovingly. That is your God.

Step #8: Splitting of an Animal

As part of the covenant-cutting ceremony, the contract was not the only thing to get cut — animals would get cut. In two. We saw an example of this at the Abrahamic covenant cutting (Gen. 15:9–10).

This demonstrated the solemnity of the ceremony. Furthermore, an oath would be taken while the two covenant partners would stand between the two dead animals asking God to do to them what had just happened to these two animals if they broke the covenant. It is as if they were saying, "God, kill me if I break this covenant."

Who Died?

The animal that died to cut the New Covenant was "the Lamb of God who takes away the sin of the world" (John 1:29).

Do We Die?

Having concluded this, that **one died for all**, therefore all died; and **He died** for all, so that they who live might **no longer live for themselves**, but for Him who died and rose again on their behalf. . . . Therefore if anyone is in Christ, he is a new creature; the **old things passed away**; behold, new things have come (2 Cor. 5:14–17).

For through the Law **I died** to the Law, so that I might live to God. I have been crucified with Christ; and it is **no longer I who live**, but **Christ lives in me**; and the life which **I now live** in the flesh I live by faith in the Son of God, who loved me and **gave Himself up for me** (Gal. 2:19–20).

The Christian walk is not about fulfillment; it is about death to self and new life in Christ. If you are following a preacher who promises "your best life now," run. The only way you can live your best life now is if you plan on going to hell. Our best life is yet to come in heaven.

In this life, we are only promised trials, tribulations, temptation, and persecution (John 16:33; 2 Tim. 3:12). This life is not about happiness, it is about holiness. This life is about dying to our carnal, selfish, sinful desires and living for the One who died for us.

Step #9: Walking through the Pieces or the Walk of Death

After pieces of the sacrificial animal were laid opposite one another, the covenanting partners would walk between those pieces, signifying a walk into death. This walk into death was a testimony of their intention to die to their own independent living. Now they were to always live in consideration of the other person.

Is there a new covenant "walk of death?" Absolutely.

The ark of the covenant in the Holy of Holies of God's tabernacle represented the throne of God. Only on the Day of Atonement was the priest allowed to go into the Holy of Holies and put the blood of the sacrifice on the mercy seat of the ark of the covenant. The people themselves could not enter the Holy of Holies to be in the presence of God; the veil shut them out.

Do you remember what happened to the veil when Jesus died as a scapegoat outside of the city?

> And behold, the **veil of the temple was torn** in two from top to bottom; and the earth shook and the rocks were split (Matt. 27:51).

What does that mean to us? What does that symbolize?

> Therefore, brethren, since we have confidence **to enter the holy places** by the blood of Jesus, by a new and living way which He inaugurated for us **through the veil, that is, His flesh** (Heb. 10:19–20).

Jesus Christ, the Lamb of God, was split for us that we might walk though Him and have direct access to the Father. No more outer courtyard. Because of Jesus, we are brought into an intimate relationship with the Father.

> Jesus said to him, "I am the way, and the truth, and the life; no one comes to the Father but through Me" (John 14:6).

Step #10: The Covenant Meal

When the cutting of the covenant was complete, a special covenant meal would follow. At this meal, each partner would feed the other. At this point you are no doubt seeing the parallels between ancient covenant ceremonies and modern-day weddings.

> - A walk of death as you walk down the aisle between your family and the in-laws. Just kidding. Maybe.
> - Two become one.
> - An oath to remain faithful "till death do you part"
> - A visible seal of the covenant: your wedding ring
> - A covenant meal with overpriced chicken
> - Feeding cake to one another

There are two differences in the old covenant meal and the modern ceremony.

1. In the old days, when covenant partners would feed each other, they would not smash the food into their covenant partner's face. What's up with that, anyway?

2. In the old days, they did not feed one another cake. At the covenant meal, a piece of bread was dipped into wine and then fed to their covenant partner. The bread represented their body and the wine their blood. This was symbolically saying, "I am giving you my life."

Consider what Jesus said when He shared His last supper with His disciples.

The Lord Jesus in the night in which He was betrayed **took bread**; and when He had given thanks, He broke it and said, "**This is My body, which is for you**; do this in remembrance of Me." In the same way He took the cup also after supper, saying, "This cup is **the new covenant in My blood**; do this, as often as you drink it, in remembrance of Me" (1 Cor. 11:23–25).

Are You in the Covenant?

Why did you become a Christian? How did you become a Christian? Were you aware of the demands of becoming a Christian prior to confessing faith?

And He was saying to them all, "If anyone wishes to come after Me, he must **deny himself**, and **take up his cross daily** and **follow Me**. For whoever wishes to save his life will lose it, but whoever loses his life for My sake, he is the one who will save it. For what is a man profited if he gains the whole world, and loses or forfeits himself? For whoever is ashamed of Me and My words, the Son of Man will be ashamed of him when He comes in His glory, and the glory of the Father and of the holy angels (Luke 9:23–26).

Did you know that Jesus asks you to die to yourself and live for Him? Did you know that following Jesus will cost you everything? Did you know that you must be willing to forsake everything to gain eternity?

None of your sacrifices earn you a single thing. Instead, you should be willing to sacrifice everything because Jesus sacrificed Himself for you. You do not earn salvation by dying to self, but you should be willing to die to yourself because He died for you.

What does Jesus demand? Repentance.

Repentance

Unfortunately, the word "repent" is rarely used in churches these days. That is unfortunate, because the New Testament commands us to repent 30 times. Some people ignore the word altogether, others offer an incorrect definition.

The Greek word for repentance is *metanoia*. It literally means: change of mind. That transliterated meaning has led too many to claim that repentance is a mere change of mind. That falls far short of Jesus' words and the biblical use of the word *metanoia*.

Imagine a man who committed adultery against his wife. He gets busted. He is bummed. He returns home, empty-handed, and announces to his wife, "I have changed my mind about you. I am coming home."

If that wife had a frying pan handy, I suspect that fellow would have it applied directly to the top of his head. A change of mind is appropriate, but hardly adequate.

You Can't Do That

Some people say that a person can't turn from their sins; it's impossible. No, it's not.

For starters, repentance is a gift from God (Acts 11:18). Second of all, with the right information, a person most certainly can repent.

If you love chocolate and someone you respect told you to "repent of your chocolate," you might give it up for a while; but as soon as you saw a Godiva Truffle, you would backslide. Fast.

But if you discovered that someone took DNA from your fingerprints on this book and ran them through some tests and the tests concluded, beyond the shadow of a doubt, that chocolate will kill you, you would give up chocolate. Fast.

You might still desire chocolate. You might even occasionally slip and sneak a Hershey Kiss, but you will have turned from your chocolate and given it up. That is repentance — new attitude toward the things you once loved and a desire for things you once hated.

Direction, Not Perfection

Don't hear that you are going to be perfect. You are not. Repentance is not about perfection, but a new direction. You will never be perfect on this side of the veil, but you will have new desires to die to self and live for Him.

Sanctification

When a man or woman repents and trusts Jesus, that person is once and for all seen as righteous. You are not just seen as forgiven, but you are seen as holy. Justification is a one-time declarative act from heaven where God says, "Totally forgiven, justified, and righteous."

At salvation, you are forever justified and righteous, but then you begin the process of actually becoming holy. You are forever justified, but you are not completely sanctified until you get to heaven.

> For those whom He foreknew, He also predestined to **become conformed** to the image of His Son, so that He would be the first-born among many brethren; and these whom He **predestined**, He also **called**; and these whom He called, He also **justified**; and these whom He justified, He also **glorified** (Rom. 8:29–30).

It's a Work

Some people say that repentance is a work. No, it is not.

Imagine a man who was hit by a truck and left in the street to die. With his last ounce of strength he was able to use his cell phone to call 911. An ambulance appeared and resuscitated him. Would anyone say that he saved himself? No! His phone call did not save him — the paramedics saved him. The same thing is true with repentance.

Repentance does not save — Jesus saves. Repentance is merely the right response to the great news that there is someone who will rescue you from your peril.

Six Steps

Imagine that you and a friend were in Omaha and your pal says, "Hey, let's drive to Florida. I'll drive. I know the way."

You hop in his car and start driving. Ten hours go by and you start to get concerned. As you drive by a bank, you notice the temperature is cooler than when you left Omaha. Strange, it should be getting warmer as you drive south.

Then you notice that you are not seeing palm trees. Instead, you are seeing more and more pine trees. Odd.

All of a sudden you see a sign that reads, "Canada: 84 miles." That's it, you know you are going in the wrong direction. What do you want your buddy to do?

Undoubtedly you would like him to do more than "change his mind." You would want him to:

1. Agree with you, "We are headed in the wrong direction."
2. You would not want him to agree with you and keep on driving. You would want him to stop.
3. You would want him to ask for your forgiveness.

4. You would not want to just sit there, you would want him to turn around.

5. You would not want him to just turn around, you would want him to start driving in the right direction.

6. You would not want him to stop until you get to your destination.

THAT is biblical repentance!

Have You Repented?

Have you seen the seriousness of your sin? Have you seen the sacrifice of the Savior who loves you? Have you turned from your sins, asked for His forgiveness and placed your trust in Jesus alone?

There are many who will cry out to Jesus on the day of judgment, "Lord, Lord." And He will respond, "I never knew you" (Matt. 7:21–23). It is not enough to know Jesus; you must be known by Him, and He will know you and welcome you if, and only if, you come to Him now in repentance and faith.

Having heard the serious nature of entering a covenant and Jesus' sobering demands on those who will follow after Him, are you certain you are in a covenant relationship with Jesus Christ?

> Perhaps you once uttered a simple "sinner's prayer," but have you repented?
> Perhaps you once walked an aisle to "accept Jesus," but have you repented?
> Perhaps you "asked Jesus into your heart," but have you repented?
> Perhaps you were "confirmed," but have you repented?
> Perhaps you were baptized as a baby, but have you repented?

If you would have forgiveness and everlasting life, here are the terms of the contract: repentance and faith in Jesus.

There is no lawyer who can change the terms. You will not have an attorney when you stand before God to be judged. You will stand alone before God alone. Have you repented and trusted His Son? Are you in covenant with the King?

Yes, I Am

If you are safely in the new covenant with God, then you have a banquet to look forward to. You can look forward to an amazing celebratory feast.

When Jesus ate His last Passover meal, He promised that He would not drink from the last cup of the feast until He returned (Matt. 26:27–29). When He returns and judges the earth, Jesus will then dine with those He has saved.

When Jesus' enemies are vanquished and death reigns no more, we will dine with Him in celebration (Rev. 19:9). You will never guess who will be the servants at this magnificent celebratory meal.

Will we have to serve ourselves? No. Will unsaved people serve us? Nope. Will it be the really bad people from history, like Hitler or Stalin or Genghis Khan? Nope. Will it be the angels or demons? No and no. Will the devil himself be the servant at the great feast? No.

Jesus Will Serve Us

The King of kings and Lord of lords, in typical humble fashion, will serve those who should be the servants. The Master of the palace will again humble Himself to wait on the ones He purchased with His own blood (Luke 12:35–37).

This is almost beyond our comprehension. Instead of insisting on being served, the Lord Almighty serves us. The King serves the servants. The owner serves the owned. The master serves His slaves. The Creator serves His creation. Unfathomable.

There is no other god who is so kind. There is no other god that is so humble. There is no other god that is so good. There is no other god.

You Are Not in the Covenant

If you have not died to yourself that you might be born again, what must you do? Let the Law "kill you" (Rom. 7:11). The Law of God was given to crush you and your pride so that God can make you alive again.

The laws of Moses were given to lead you to Jesus Christ (Gal. 3:24). The laws were intended to drive you to His feet and call out, "I can't. I can't keep your laws. I have broken your laws in thought, word, and deed. Please, save me from the wrath that is to come."

How does the Law kill you and lead you to Jesus? Open it up and let it be a mirror that allows you to see yourself in truth. Let the Law reveal to you what you look like, not in your imagination, but to God.

When Jesus preached the Sermon on the Mount, He was opening up the Law to His hearers. Let Him open up the law for you as you examine yourself in light of God's perfect standard.

"You have heard that the ancients were told, 'You shall not commit murder' and 'Whoever commits murder shall be liable to the court.' **But I say** to you that everyone who is angry with his brother shall be guilty before the court; and whoever says to his brother, 'You good-for-nothing,' shall be guilty before the supreme court; and whoever says, 'You fool,' shall be guilty enough to go into **the fiery hell**" (Matt. 5:21–22).

Are you a murderer at heart? You are if you have ever been unjustly angry with anyone. Have you ever yelled at your kids? Have you ever said nasty things to your spouse? Have you ever flipped off another driver? Congrats. God sees you as a murderer.

"You have heard that it was said, 'You shall not commit adultery'; but I say to you that everyone who looks at a woman with lust for her has already committed **adultery with her in his heart**" (Matt. 5:27–28).

Ever ogled someone? Ever fantasized? Ever read a "romance" novel? Ever looked at porn? You are an adulterer at heart in the eyes of God. Nobody knows your thought life. Except God.

"You have heard that it was said, 'You shall love your neighbor and hate your enemy.' But I say to you, love your enemies and pray for those who persecute you" (Matt. 5:43–44).

The world loves love. The world is happy to tell you to love. After all, it is what the world needs now. But love is not a nice sentimental emotion. Love is a law. Love is a command.

Perhaps you think you have been a loving person, but have you loved your enemies? Have you loved them the way you love yourself? More than that, have you loved God with all of your heart, soul, mind, and strength?

[Jesus said,] "You shall love the Lord your God **with all your heart**, and with **all your soul**, and with **all your mind**." This is the great and foremost commandment. The second is like it, "You shall love your neighbor as yourself" (Matt. 22:37–39).

Have you been fully devoted to loving everyone you meet? Have you sacrificed your life in the service of others? Have you worshiped God every second of every day?

Are you starting to feel the weight of the Law?

Jesus does not let up. In the Sermon on the Mount, He insists that only perfect people will go to heaven. In the beatitudes, He claims that only those who are perfectly humble, perfectly mourn for their sins, are perfectly gentle, who perfectly strive to be righteous, who are perfectly merciful and pure in heart will inherit the Kingdom of God (Matt. 5:3–11).

Perhaps you have heard atheists, or even some Christians, suggest that Jesus was just a good teacher who taught us to love one another. Hardly. Jesus was certainly a good teacher, but His words were hard. He not only demanded perfection in the inward places, He demanded perfection of our thought life or we would be cast into hell. Hardly the words of a "nice guy." These are the words of a demanding and perfect God.

Jesus' standard is an unattainable standard. Do you see your need for a Savior? Do you see how far short you have fallen? Do you see your plight?

> Therefore, we are ambassadors for Christ, as though God were making an appeal through us; **we beg you** on behalf of Christ, **be reconciled to God**. He made Him who knew no sin to be sin on our behalf, so that we might become the righteousness of God **in Him**. . . .
> He says,
> "At the acceptable time I listened to you,
> And on the day of salvation I helped you."
> Behold, **now** is "the acceptable time," behold, **now** is "the day of salvation" ((2 Cor 5:20–6:2).

You cannot save yourself. But He stands ready to forgive you.

All of the work has been done for you. The Lord offers to be your covenant partner and forgive you and offer you the kingdom.

Today is the day of salvation. Repent and believe in Jesus. Now.

> *Jesus clearly equates Himself with God.*
> *There is nothing vague about His claims.*

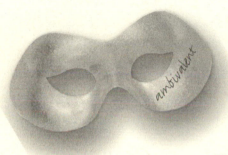

Chapter 20

Jesus Is the I AM

Abraham Lincoln versus Frederick Douglass: child's play.

Richard Nixon versus John F. Kennedy: trivial

Tom Cruise versus Jack Nicholson: small potatoes.

The greatest debate of all time took place two thousand years ago in Jerusalem. The opponents: Jesus and the Pharisees. The subject: deity. Was Jesus really God in flesh?

Four Accounts

If you have ever wondered why we have four Gospel accounts of the life of Jesus, there are many reasons.

1. Each Gospel offers a slightly different perspective of the same events. If you have ever wondered why one account says "one man was healed" while another account says "two men were healed," it is because each Gospel is talking about the same story from a different perspective and reporting different details. You

see this on the news all the time. One station will say that two people were killed in a crash while another says that two people were killed and four injured. Is one of the reporters wrong? Nope, they are just reporting the story from a different perspective.

2. Multiple eyewitness accounts encourage us that the life of Jesus is not the mere hallucination of just one author.

3. Each Gospel is written to a different group of people.

> Matthew is written to Jews.
> Mark is written to Gentiles.
> Luke was written to a Gentile leader.
> John was written to the world.

4. Each Gospel is written with a different emphasis.

> Matthew is written to show that Jesus is King.
> Mark is written to show Jesus as the suffering servant.
> Luke is written to show that Jesus is the Son of Man.
> John is written to show that Jesus is God.

Therefore many other **signs** Jesus also performed in the presence of the disciples, which are not written in this book; but these have been written so that you may believe that Jesus is the Christ, the **Son of God**; and that believing **you may have life** in His name (John 20:30–31).

Ego Eimi

We have seen many different types and shadows and fuzzy pictures of Jesus. Each one of these types has been lesser than the anti-type, Jesus. John shows us one "type" in the Old Testament that is not less than Jesus. John used God as a picture of Jesus to prove that Jesus is indeed, God.

Then Moses said to God, "Behold, I am going to the sons of Israel, and I will say to them, 'The God of your fathers has sent me to you.' Now they may say to me, '**What is His name?**' What shall I say to them?"

God said to Moses, "**I AM WHO I AM**"; and He said, "Thus you shall say to the sons of Israel, '**I AM** has sent me to you.' "

God, furthermore, said to Moses, "Thus you shall say to the sons of Israel, 'The LORD, the God of your fathers, the God of Abraham, the God of Isaac, and the God of Jacob, has sent me to you.'

This is My name forever, and this is My memorial-name to all generations" (Exod. 3:13–15).

The name that God gave to Moses identifies Him as the eternal, self-existent, never changing, "I AM." The Hebrew word *YAHWEH* is used to identify Him as the One who was, is, and is to come (Exod. 3:14).

The Greek version of the Old Testament, called the Septuagint, uses the Greek words *ego eimi* (I am) for the Hebrew word *YAHWEH*. In English, we use the words, I AM.

The New Testament is written in Greek, and in the Gospel of John, we see Jesus refer to Himself as "I AM" no less than 21 times. We have already seen many of these "I AM" statements.

> I am the door (John 10:9).
> I am the living water (John 7:37–39).
> I am the light of the world (John 8:12).
> I am the way (John 14:6).
> I am the bread of life (John 6:35).

Unfortunately, the English translation of the Greek Bible does not have the same impact as the original language. So here are a few "I AM" statements transliterated for you, that is, the word-for-word translation of the original Greek. The word order of Jesus' "I AM" statements makes it clear that He was proclaiming Himself to be the Always Existing One. Notice how Jesus says, "I AM" at the end of the sentence to emphasize what He was trying to say.

1. Jesus was preaching in the temple in John 8:24.

   English: "Therefore I said to you that you will die in your sins; for unless you believe that **I am He**, you will die in your sins.

   Greek: I say then to you that you will die in the sins of you; if for not you might trust that *Ego Eimi*."

2. Jesus still doing open air at the temple in John 8:28.

   English: So Jesus said, "When you lift up the Son of Man, then you will know that **I am He**, and I do nothing on My own initiative, but I speak these things as the Father taught Me."

   Greek: Said then to them the Jesus, "When you might elevate the son of the man, then you will know that *Ego Eimi*."

3. John 8:58: Jesus still preaching at the temple in John 8:58.

> **English:** Jesus said to them, "Truly, truly, I say to you, before Abraham was born, **I am**."
>
> **Greek:** Said to them Jesus, "Amen, amen I say to you, before Abraham to become, *Ego Eimi*."

Upon hearing Him say, "Before Abraham was, *EGO EIMI*," the Jews were so infuriated that He equated Himself with God, they tried to stone Him (John 8:59). Jesus' hearers were not confused that He was claiming to be God.

Even More

There are more examples of Jesus' clear claim to deity in the Gospel of John.

4. Jesus walked on the water and the disciples were afraid in John 6:20.

> **English:** But he said to them, "It is I; do not be afraid."
> **Greek:** The One but says to them, "*Ego Eimi*. Not fear."

5. Jesus at the Passover meal in John 13:19.

> **English:** From now on I am telling you before it comes to pass, so that when it does occur, you may believe that **I am He**.
> **Greek:** "From now I say to you before the to become, that you might trust when it might become because, *Ego Eimi*."

6. Jesus in the Garden of Gethsemane in John 18:4–5.

> **English:** So Jesus, knowing all the things that were coming upon Him, went forth and said to them, "Whom do you seek?" They answered Him, "Jesus the Nazarene." He said to them, "**I am He**." And Judas also, who was betraying Him, was standing with them.
> **Greek:** "Whom seek you?"
> "They answered to him, "Jesus the Nazarene."
> He says to them, "*Ego Eimi*."
> You get the point. Twenty-one times Jesus equates Himself with God Himself.

Bonus for Jehovah's Witnesses

Sadly, Jehovah's Witnesses don't study Greek. If they did, they would know that the Gospel of John makes it abundantly clear: Jesus is God.

Jehovah's Witnesses like to say, "The first verse of John doesn't use a definite article to prove that Jesus is THE God, but it simply says that Jesus is A God. Wrong.

John 1:1, New American Standard Bible: In the beginning was the Word, and the Word was with God, and the Word was God.

John 1:1, New World (Jehovah's Witnesses) Translation: In [the] beginning the Word was, and the Word was with God, and the Word was a god.

John 1:1, original Greek, word for word: In beginning was the word, and the word was toward the God, and **God was the Word**.

The Greek word order is emphatically clear: God was the Word. Jesus is the Word; therefore, Jesus is God.

Clearer Than a Type

Jesus clearly equates Himself with God. There is nothing vague about His claims.

Jesus was so clear on this, the Jews wanted to stone him (John 8:59) and they ultimately crucified Him for "claiming to be God" (Matt. 26:63–66).

Jesus is God. Jesus is the Truth. What are you going to do with that knowledge?

You Protest

Perhaps you are thinking, "Okay, so Jesus equated Himself with the God of the Old Testament, big deal! The God of the Old Testament never claimed to be the only true and living God."

Are you sure?

Not only did God make exclusive claims of divinity in the first commandment (You shall have no other gods before Me), but He actually mocked other so-called deities. If you think God was never sarcastic, brace yourself for mocking satire from God.

Thus says the LORD,

"Do not learn the way of the nations,
And do not be terrified by the signs of the heavens

Although the nations are terrified by them;
For **the customs of the peoples are delusion**;
Because it is wood cut from the forest,
The work of the hands of a craftsman with a cutting tool.
They decorate it with silver and with gold;
They fasten it with nails and with hammers
So that it will not totter.
Like a scarecrow in a cucumber field are they,
And they cannot speak;
They **must be carried**,
Because they cannot walk!
Do not fear them,
For they can do no harm,
Nor can they do any good."

There is none like You, O Lord;
You are great, and great is Your name in might.
Who would not fear You, O King of the nations?
Indeed it is Your due!
For among all the wise men of the nations
And in all their kingdoms,
There is none like You.
But they are altogether **stupid and foolish**
In their discipline of delusion — their idol is wood!
Beaten silver is brought from Tarshish,
And gold from Uphaz,
The work of a craftsman and of the hands of a goldsmith;
Violet and purple are their clothing;
They are all the work of skilled men.
But the Lord is the true God;
He is the living God and the everlasting King.
At His wrath the earth quakes,
And the nations cannot endure His indignation.

Thus you shall say to them, "The gods that did not make the heavens and the earth will perish from the earth and from under the heavens."

It is He who **made the earth** by His power,
Who **established the world** by His wisdom;

And by His understanding He has stretched out the heavens.
When He utters His voice, there is a tumult of waters in
    the heavens,
And He causes the clouds to ascend from the end of
    the earth;
He makes lightning for the rain,
And brings out the wind from His storehouses.
Every man is stupid, devoid of knowledge;
Every goldsmith is put to shame by his idols;
For his **molten images are deceitful**,
And there is **no breath in them**.
They are **worthless**, a work of mockery;
In the time of their punishment they will perish.
The portion of Jacob is not like these;
For the Maker of all is He,
And Israel is the tribe of His inheritance;
The LORD of hosts is His name (Jer. 10:2–16).

Theology Math

The God of the Old Testament claimed to be the only true and living God.
    Jesus equated Himself with the God of the Old Testament.
    Therefore, Jesus is the only true and living God.
    Postmoderns claim that Jesus is "a way." Jesus does not agree.

250	⊙
	← A.D. 33: Jesus crucified
	← A.D. 30: Jesus begins ministry
	← A.D. 26: John the Baptist begins preaching
0	⊙ ← 0: Jesus is born
	← 397–5 B.C.: The silent years
250	⊙
	← 397 B.C.: Malachi is Israel's last prophet until John the Baptist
500	⊙ ← 515 B.C.: Jerusalem rebuilt and temple completed
	← 536 B.C.: Jews start returning to Jerusalem
	← 586 B.C.: Southern Kingdom falls to Babylon
750	⊙ ← 721 B.C.: Northern Kingdom falls to Assyria
	← 975 B.C.: Israel split in two
1000	⊙ ← 1004 B.C.: Solomon's temple completed
	← 1015 B.C.: Solomon becomes king
	← 1055 B.C.: David becomes king
1250	⊙
	← 1451 B.C.: The Jews enter the Promised Land
	← 1491–1451 B.C.: The Jews wander the desert
1500	⊙ ← 1491 B.C.: Moses leads the Exodus out of Egypt
	← 1700–1574 B.C.: Joseph and his brothers have lots of babies
1750	⊙ ← 1739 B.C.: Joseph sold into slavery in Egypt
	← 1836 B.C.: Jacob born
	← 1896 B.C.: Isaac born
2000	⊙ ← 1996 B.C. Abraham born
2250	⊙
	← 2349 B.C.: Noah and the Global Flood
2500	⊙
2750	⊙
3000	⊙
3250	⊙
3500	⊙
3750	⊙
4000	⊙
	← 4004 B.C.: Creation, Adam and Eve, Cain and Abel

Timeline
4004 B.C. — A.D. 33

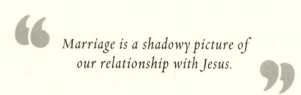

*Marriage is a shadowy picture of
our relationship with Jesus.*

Chapter 21

Jesus Is the Bridegroom

You are cordially invited to three weddings. Don't panic, you don't have to bring a gift or endure awkward toasts.

As you attend the first wedding in human history, you will discover why you are married and what the purpose of marriage is.

As you attend a first-century wedding, you will see how the Bible uses marriage as a picture of Jesus.

As for the third wedding, you are cordially invited, but you may or may not be attending it.

The First Wedding

God finished creating everything and saw that it was good. Adam, God's representative on earth, "gave names to all the cattle, and to the birds of the sky, and to every beast of the field, but for Adam there was not found a helper suitable for him" (Gen. 2:20).

God saw that "It is not good for the man to be alone; I will make him a **helper** suitable for him" (Gen. 2:18). Men are not good alone. Men are better with a suitable helper, and that suitable helper is a woman. There are two important lessons here:

1. It is not a second-class role to be a "helper." God uses the same word to describe Himself as the "helper of Israel" (Ps. 115:9–11; Hosea 13:9; Isa. 41).
2. Woman is the best companion for man. Buddies are good to have, but women are the ideal lifelong companions for fellas.

As God presented Adam's new mate to him, we hear the first recorded words of man. These words were actually Adam's wedding vows. See if they sound familiar to you.

> The man said,
>> "This is now **bone of my bones**,
>> And **flesh of my flesh**;
>> She shall be called Woman,
>> Because she was taken out of Man."
> For this reason **a man shall leave his father and his mother**, and be **joined** to his wife; and they shall become **one flesh**. And the man and his wife were both naked and were not ashamed (Gen. 2:23–25).

Your wedding vows alluded to the first wedding vows:

> Two shall become one flesh.
> "Till death do you part" comes from being "joined together," which is to cleave to one another until you die.

The Hebrew word for "man" means "hard one"; the Hebrew word for "woman" means "soft one." We complement each other and are equal in God's eyes (Gal. 3:28), but we are unmistakably different. Woman is the nurturer by design and man is the worker and provider by design.

What's the Point?

There are five reasons God created marriage:

1. Procreation. We are supposed to "be fruitful and multiply" (Gen. 1:28).
2. Sex (Song of Sol.).
3. Companionship (Gen. 2:18).

4. We do better together than apart (Gen. 2:18).
5. Marriage was created as a picture of something greater (Eph. 5).

In creating marriage, God gives us a shadowy earthly picture (type) of our relationship with Jesus. In a marriage, the man plays the role of Jesus and the woman plays the role of His Bride, the Church (Eph. 5:22–24). Clearly, marriage was created by God to be an analogy.

When a man and woman get married, they are taking the stage of a great big cosmic play. When the two players play their parts correctly, the world can look at them and understand how Jesus loves the Church and vice versa.

Marriage is a shadowy picture of our relationship with Jesus. Jesus is the Bridegroom and His Church is the Bride (Matt. 9:15; 2 Cor. 11:2).

New Testament Weddings

Prepare to attend a wedding in the first century A.D. By the time Jesus walked this earth, the Jewish wedding ceremony had been expanded from Adam's few simple words to a lengthy custom that was vivid with symbolism. The Bible uses the imagery of a first-century marriage to describe Jesus and His relationship to His Bride, the Church.

First-Century Jewish Wedding

1. **The bridal selection or *shiddukhin* was made by the father and a matchmaker.**

   > Blessed be the God and Father of our Lord Jesus Christ, who has blessed us with every spiritual blessing in the heavenly places in Christ, just as He **chose us** in Him **before the foundation of the world**, that we would be holy and blameless before Him. In love **He predestined us** to adoption as sons through Jesus Christ to Himself, according to the kind intention of His will, to the praise of the glory of His grace, which He freely bestowed on us in the Beloved (Eph. 1:3–6).

2. **A legal contract/covenant or *ketubah*.** In this contract, the groom promised to care for his wife and give himself for her. The bride promises to pay her dowry — her financial status.

   > For you have been **bought with a price**: therefore glorify God in **your body** (1 Cor. 6:20).

3. **The bridal payment or *mohar*** was paid by the groom to the bride's family. This set her free from her parents' household to be with the groom. We see an example of that with Isaac and Rebecca in Genesis 24:53 and Jacob and his wives in Genesis 29:20, 27. We are told in 1 Corinthians 6:19–20 that we have been purchased, redeemed with a price.

> . . . you were not **redeemed** with perishable things like silver or gold from your futile way of life inherited from your forefathers, but with **precious blood**, as of a lamb unblemished and spotless, the blood of Christ (1 Pet. 1:18–19).

4. **The Betrothal or *Eyrusin* or *kiddushim***, meaning sanctification or set apart. This was a time for the couple to prepare to enter into the covenant/marriage. This is much stronger than an engagement; a breaking of the betrothal was only available to the husband through divorce (Deut. 24:1–4).

    God hates divorce (Mal. 2:16) because it ruins the picture of God's relationship to us. To get a divorce is to confuse the world about the gospel and God's relationship with His people. When God pays for us and unites us to Himself, He commits for life. God never "divorces" us.

> I give **eternal** life to them, and they will **never** perish; and **no one** will snatch them out of My hand (John 10:28).

    God has married you to His Son. You cannot divorce Him and He will not divorce you.

5. **The betrothal ceremony**: the bride and groom would appear together under a *huppah* (canopy) and publicly express their intention to become engaged. The canopy symbolized a new household being planned (referred to in Ps. 19:5 and Joel 2:16). An item of value would be exchanged (such as rings) and a cup of wine was shared to seal the vows.

> And when He [Jesus] had taken a **cup** and given thanks, He gave it to them, saying, "Drink from it, all of you; for this is My blood **of the covenant**, which is poured out for many for forgiveness of sins. But I say to you, I **will not drink** of this fruit of the vine from now on **until that day** when I drink it new with you in My Father's kingdom" (Matt. 26:27–29).

6. **The betrothal period** was to last one year and the couple was considered married, but were not intimate. They lived separately until the end of the betrothal period. Joseph and Mary are a good example of this in Matthew 1:18–25.

> Little children, I am with you a little while longer. You will seek Me; and as I said to the Jews, now I also say to you, "Where I am going, **you cannot come**" (John 13:33).

7. **After the betrothal ceremony**, the groom would return home to fulfill his obligations during the betrothal. Before he left the bride at the betrothal ceremony, the groom would leave a gift as a reminder that he would return to receive her.

> You were sealed in Him with **the Holy Spirit of promise**, who is given **as a pledge** of our inheritance, with a view to the redemption of God's own possession, to the praise of His glory (Eph. 1:13–14).

8. **During the betrothal**, the groom was to focus on preparing a dwelling place for the bride. Typically this was done not by building a new dwelling, but by adding a room to his existing home. The rabbis determined that this was to be a better place than what she had been living in. The groom would not decide when the place was ready, but his father would make the determination and give the go-ahead to receive the bride.

> In My Father's house are many dwelling places; if it were not so, I would have told you; for **I go** to prepare a place for you. If I go and prepare a place for you, **I will come again** and **receive you** to Myself, that where I am, there you may be also (John 14:2–3).

> But of that day and hour **no one knows**, not even the angels of heaven, **nor the Son**, but the Father alone (Matt. 24:36).

9. **During the betrothal** the bride was to keep herself busy for the wedding day by preparing wedding garments.

> For you yourselves know full well that the day of the Lord will come just like a thief in the night. . . . so then let us not sleep as—others do, but let us **be alert and sober** (1 Thess. 5:2–6).

Be on the alert then, for you do not know the day nor the hour (Matt. 25:13).

While the bridegroom was preparing their new dwelling, the bride was to be preparing herself so she could be presented "in all her glory, having no spot or wrinkle or any such thing; but that she would be holy and blameless" (Eph. 5:27).

10. **The wedding day** was a surprise to the bride. Remember, the father of the groom determined when everything was ready. A member of the bridegroom's party would appear at the bride's house and shout, "Behold, the bridegroom comes." Then a shofar horn would blow, announcing the arrival of the groom.

For the Lord Himself will descend from heaven **with a shout**, with the voice of the archangel and with **the trumpet of God**, and the dead in Christ will rise first (1 Thess. 4:16).

11. The entire party would come with the groom and the bride and groom would go under the *huppah* (to establish a new household), they would say a blessing over the cup of wine, and the ceremony would include final vows. The pinnacle of the ceremony was the marriage supper, at least seven days of celebration. When it was all done, the groom would bring his bride home in a full covenant marriage.

And the armies which are in heaven, clothed in fine linen, white and clean, **were following Him** on white horses (Rev. 19:14).

And He will send forth His angels with a great trumpet and they will gather together **His elect** from the four winds, from one end of the sky to the other (Matt. 24:31).

Blessed are those who are invited to the **marriage supper** of the Lamb (Rev. 19:9).

Cross references:
Revelation 19:14 : Rev 19:8
Revelation 19:14 : Rev 3:4; 19:8

12. The new couple would then dwell in their **new home**, which was not new, but improved.

Then I saw a **new heaven** and a **new earth**; for the first heaven and the first earth passed away, and there is no longer any sea. And I saw the holy city, **new Jerusalem**, coming down out of heaven from God, made ready as a bride adorned for her husband.

And I heard a loud voice from the throne, saying, "Behold, the **tabernacle** of God is among men, and He will **dwell among them**, and they shall be His people, and God Himself will be **among them**, and He will wipe away every tear from their eyes; and there will no longer be any death; there will no longer be any mourning, or crying, or pain; the first things have passed away" (Rev. 21:1–4).

You Have Responded to the Wedding Invitation

At the final wedding, you are not only going to attend the celebration, you are actually going to be a gift. At the wedding celebration of the Lamb, God the Father is going to give a gift to God the Son: the Church. If you are a believer in the Lord Jesus Christ, you have been purchased by the Father as a gift for the Son (1 Cor. 15).

When someone says, "I love Jesus but I hate the Church," that is like saying to a man, "I like you but I hate your wife." You can't love one and hate the other.

If you have been married to Jesus through repentance and faith, you can look forward to His return, anticipating a great feast and spending eternity with the One who will make all things new.

> No more sorrow.
> No more pain.
> No more cancer.
> No more children dying.
> No more starvation.
> No more divorce.
> No more mental illness.
> No more depression.
> No more prodigal children.
> No more adultery.
> No more pornography.
> No more sin.

Parable of the Marriage Feast

If you have not responded to the exceedingly good news of the Gospel, Jesus describes the final wedding of all time.

> Jesus spoke to them again in parables, saying, "The kingdom of heaven may be compared to a **king who gave a wedding feast for his son**. And he sent out his slaves to call those who had been invited to the **wedding feast**, and they were **unwilling to come**. Again he sent out other slaves saying, 'Tell those who have been invited, "Behold, **I have prepared my dinner**; my oxen and my fattened livestock are all butchered and everything is ready; **come to the wedding feast**." '
>
> "But they **paid no attention** and went their way, one to his own farm, another to his business, and the rest seized his slaves and mistreated them and killed them. But **the king was enraged**, and he sent his armies and destroyed those murderers and set their city on fire.
>
> "Then he said to his slaves, 'The wedding is ready, but those who were invited were not worthy. Go therefore to the main highways, and as many as you find there, **invite to the wedding feast**.' Those slaves went out into the streets and gathered together all they found, both evil and good; and the wedding hall was filled with dinner guests" (Matt. 22:1–11).

It is God's desire to save you (1 Tim. 2:4). He has prepared a banquet for you. Has anyone ever sent you a more fantastic invitation? In order to attend, you must respond in repentance and faith in Jesus Christ exclusively. If you do not, if you try to sneak into the banquet with good works or believing that Jesus is simply "a way," the parable of the wedding feast continues for you.

> "But when the king came in to look over the dinner guests, he saw a man there who was **not dressed in wedding clothes**, and he said to him, 'Friend, how did you come in here without wedding clothes?' And the man was speechless. Then the king said to the servants, 'Bind him hand and foot, and **throw him into the outer darkness**; in that place there will be **weeping** and **gnashing** of teeth.' For many are called, but few are chosen" (Matt. 22:11–14).

Do not be deceived, you will not sneak into heaven if you believe:

> > Jesus will save me after all I can do (Eph. 2:8–9).

> Jesus is a way, but He is not the way (John 14:6).

> Jesus was a good teacher, but He was not God (John 8:24).

Jesus does not tolerate other suitors. He has not prepared a new heaven for you to give your affection to another. Besides, why would you want to be united with anything less than the only true and living God?

Even now Jesus is preparing the great wedding feast of the Lamb. Will you not come?

> *Jesus in not merely a good teacher. Jesus is not a fable or myth. Jesus is God.*

Chapter 22

Jesus Is . . .

Who is Jesus?

He is our better Adam.

His blood speaks to us of better things than the blood of Abel.

He is a better priest in the order of Melchizedek.

His *actual* sacrifice is better than the *almost* sacrifice of Jacob.

His three days in the belly of the earth are better than Jonah's three days in the belly of the whale.

He is the perfect Prophet.

He is the highest High Priest.

He is the mightiest King.

He is the bronze serpent raised up for us, that whoever looks to Him will live. Eternally.

He is the ark of our salvation that saves us from the wrath that is to come.

He is the only door whereby we can enter heaven.

He is the ladder who takes us to heaven.

He is our city of refuge.

He is our surety, our Sabbath rest and our better Festival.

He is the Bread of Life.

He is the living water.

He is our bridegroom.

He is our Rock, our Fortress and our Deliverer.

He is our Savior and our ransom.

He is the tabernacle come down from heaven.

He is the Holy One of Israel.

He is the Great I AM.

He is the way, the truth, and the life.

He is Jesus Christ, the Lamb of God who takes away the sins of the world.

He is the One who commands you this day to repent and trust Him.

That is who Jesus is.

Jesus Unmasked

You have seen the evidence. You now know what Jesus believed about Himself. You have seen that the Bible is the supernaturally inspired Word of God.

Knowing the effort that God went through to prepare a holy nation to deliver a Messiah who would fulfill all righteousness and suffocate to death on a Cross to satisfy the wrath of God so that you might have forgiveness of sins, does it make any sense that you can get to God through jihad? Or through the teachings of the Bhagavad-Gita? Or through good works?

Is Jesus intolerant? Of course He is. And so are you!

You do not tolerate belligerence from your children. You do not tolerate your spouse having an affair. You do not tolerate your dog biting you. Neither does Jesus.

Because Jesus is indeed the way, the truth, and the life, and nobody comes to the Father but through Him, does it even make sense that other religions are optional paths? If so, Jesus should have said:

> I am the way, the truth and the life. Nobody comes to the Father except through Me. Or Mohammed. Or Joseph Smith. Or Buddha. Or whatever.

What Will You Do?

If you have eyes to see and ears to hear, it is clear, the Bible is axiomatic, and Jesus is not a preference. Jesus is not merely a good teacher. Jesus is not a fable or myth. Jesus is God.

You can humbly come before the King of kings and Lord of lords now and surrender, or you can wait until you die and meet Him face to face.

> Worship the LORD with reverence and rejoice with trembling. **Do homage to the Son**, that He not become angry, and you perish in the way, for His **wrath** may soon be kindled. How blessed are all who **take refuge** in Him! (Ps. 2:11–12).

Today, Jesus offers you terms of peace if you will come to Him in repentance and faith. If you delay, God has given Jesus the authority to "break them with a rod of iron . . . shatter them like earthenware" (Ps. 2:9). Do not trifle with King Jesus.

> Being found in appearance as a man, He **humbled Himself** by becoming obedient to the point of death, even death on a cross. For this reason also, **God highly exalted Him**, and bestowed on Him the name which is above every name, so that at the name of Jesus EVERY KNEE WILL BOW, of those who are in heaven and on earth and under the earth, and that **every tongue will confess** that Jesus Christ is Lord, to the glory of God the Father (Phil. 2:8–11).

You can bow the knee willingly to benevolent King Jesus today, or you can meet Him face to face when He is angry. Either way, you will confess that Jesus is Lord. Why would you delay?

This Is Not a Game

When Jesus came to die for you He was meek and mild. At the consummation of history He will come with His mighty angels in flaming fire.

> **The Lord Jesus** will be revealed from heaven with His **mighty angels** in **flaming fire**, dealing out retribution to those who do not know God and to those who **do not obey** the gospel of our Lord Jesus. These **will pay** the penalty of **eternal destruction**, away from the presence of the Lord and from the glory of His power, when He comes **to be glorified in His saints** on that day, and to be marveled at among all who have believed — for our testimony to you was believed (2 Thess. 1:7–10).

That is the Unmasked Jesus. The Unmasked Jesus is the Creator, Savior, and Conquering King.

You can prefer whatever ice cream you choose, but Jesus is not a flavor. Jesus is not merely a good teacher or a nice guy. Jesus is not a myth or mere miracle worker.

Jesus is your God and you know it. Jesus demands your allegiance. Jesus commands you this day to repent. Be reconciled to God.

Scripture Reference Guide

Genesis 1:1 // 173
Genesis 1:28 // 224
Genesis 1:31 // 33
Genesis 2:17 // 33
Genesis 2:18 // 224, 225
Genesis 2:20 // 223
Genesis 2:23-25 // 224
Genesis 3:6 // 172
Genesis 3:6-7 // 34
Genesis 3:15 // 34
Genesis 3:21 // 34
Genesis 4:3-8 // 162
Genesis 4:4-5 // 35
Genesis 5:1 // 173
Genesis 6:5-6 // 51
Genesis 6:7 // 60
Genesis 6:13-14 // 60
Genesis 6:14 // 61
Genesis 7:15-16 // 60
Genesis 9:13 // 202
Genesis 14:18 // 162
Genesis 15:12 // 186
Genesis 15:9-10 // 186, 203
Genesis 15:9-17 // 186
Genesis 17 // 65
Genesis 17:5 // 202
Genesis 17:7 // 95
Genesis 17:8 // 202
Genesis 17:9-14 // 202
Genesis 17:15 // 202
Genesis 22:12-14 // 36
Genesis 22:2 // 163
Genesis 22:5-8 // 36
Genesis 22:6 // 163
Genesis 22:7 // 163
Genesis 24:53 // 226
Genesis 28:12 // 180
Genesis 29:20 // 226
Genesis 29:27 // 226
Genesis 30:22-24 // 166
Genesis 37:2 // 166
Genesis 37:13 // 166
Genesis 37:18-20 // 166
Genesis 37:18-28 // 166
Genesis 37:26-28 // 167
Genesis 37:28 // 167
Genesis 37:3 // 166
Genesis 37:5-11 // 166

Genesis 37:6-11 // 166
Genesis 39:1 // 167
Genesis 39:3 // 167
Genesis 39:11-20 // 167
Genesis 39:21 // 167
Genesis 39:23 // 167
Genesis 40:1-3 // 167
Genesis 40:20-22 // 167
Genesis 41:38 // 167
Genesis 41:43 // 167
Genesis 41:45 // 167
Genesis 41:55-57 // 167
Genesis 42:8 // 167
Genesis 43:9 // 180
Genesis 44:32-34 // 180
Genesis 45:5-8 // 167
Genesis 45:16-20 // 167
Genesis 47:25 // 167
Genesis 50:20 // 167
Exodus 3:13-15 // 217
Exodus 3:14 // 217
Exodus 11:4-8 // 37
Exodus 12:3-13 // 37
Exodus 12:39 // 131
Exodus 12:42 // 131
Exodus 15 // 79
Exodus 15:22-25 // 67
Exodus 16:1-3 // 80
Exodus 16:4 // 80
Exodus 17 // 79
Exodus 17:1-2 // 68
Exodus 17:2 // 68
Exodus 17:2-4 // 68
Exodus 17:5-6 // 68
Exodus 17:6 // 69
Exodus 19:5-6 // 95
Exodus 20 // 123
Exodus 20:8-11 // 124
Exodus 21:32 // 167
Exodus 31:12-17 // 123
Exodus 31:13-17 // 202
Exodus 33:3 // 143
Leviticus 16:10 // 136
Leviticus 16:7-9 // 135
Leviticus 17:11 // 38
Leviticus 23:4-7 // 130
Leviticus 23:9-12 // 132
Leviticus 23:15-16 // 133

Leviticus 23:23-25 // 134
Leviticus 23:26-28 // 135
Leviticus 23:33-36 // 136
Numbers 10:9-10 // 134
Numbers 14:28 // 177
Numbers 14:34 // 143
Numbers 14:35 // 143
Numbers 21:4-5 // 85
Numbers 21:6 // 85
Numbers 21:7 // 86
Numbers 21:8-9 // 86
Numbers 24:17 // 155
Numbers 29:35 // 136
Numbers 35:6-34 // 178
Numbers 35:9-14 // 177
Deuteronomy 1:39 // 170
Deuteronomy 13:1-5 // 149
Deuteronomy 18:15 // 163
Deuteronomy 18-22 // 146
Deuteronomy 23:25 // 122
Deuteronomy 24:1-4 // 226
Deuteronomy 25:1-3 // 68
Deuteronomy 25:5-6 // 165
Deuteronomy 28 // 94
Deuteronomy 31:6 // 177
Deuteronomy 34:10-12 // 163
Ruth 3 // 165
Ruth 4 // 165
1 Samuel 8:4-5 // 153
1 Samuel 8:10-17 // 154
1 Samuel 8:18 // 154
1 Samuel 8:19-22 // 154
1 Samuel 18:3-4 // 185
2 Samuel 12:23 // 171
1 Chronicles 17:11-14 // 155
Nehemiah 1:3 // 144
Job 3:16-19 // 170
Psalm 2 // 166
Psalm 2:11-12 // 235
Psalm 2:1-12 // 166
Psalm 7:11 // 35
Psalm 16:11 // 139
Psalm 19:1-3 // 117
Psalm 19:5 // 226
Psalm 24:7-10 // 102
Psalm 34:8 // 83
Psalm 51:3 // 169

Psalm 51:5 // 169
Psalm 51:5 // 54
Psalm 51:5 // 58
Psalm 94:9 // 157
Psalm 102:27 // 58
Psalm 110:1 // 102
Psalm 110:155 // 195
Psalm 115:9-11 // 224
Psalm 119:4 // 194
Psalm 119:9 // 194
Psalm 119:18 // 195
Psalm 119:28 // 195
Psalm 119:37 // 195
Psalm 119:41 // 195
Psalm 119:45 // 195
Psalm 119:68 // 195
Psalm 119:72 // 195
Psalm 119:80 // 195
Psalm 119:89 // 195
Psalm 119:92 // 195
Psalm 119:93 // 195
Psalm 119:98 // 195
Psalm 119:103 // 195
Psalm 119:105 // 195
Psalm 119:111 // 195
Psalm 119:116 // 195
Psalm 119:127 // 195
Psalm 119:129 // 195
Psalm 119:140 // 195
Psalm 119:144 // 195
Psalm 119:151 // 195
Psalm 119:152 // 195
Psalm 119:162 // 195
Psalm 126:3 // 139
Psalm 139:13-14 // 53
Psalm 145:15 // 80
Psalm 193:8 // 53
Proverbs 3:12 // 86
Proverbs 6:1 // 180
Isaiah 7:14 // 138
Isaiah 7:16 // 171
Isaiah 9:2 // 138
Isaiah 11:9 // 137
Isaiah 12:1-3 // 75
Isaiah 12:4-6 // 75
Isaiah 41 // 224
Isaiah 46:10 // 53
Isaiah 49:6 // 137
Isaiah 53 // 29
Isaiah 53:10 // 39
Isaiah 53:2-8 // 39

Isaiah 55 // 75
Isaiah 55:1 // 76
Isaiah 55:2 // 76
Isaiah 55:6 // 76
Isaiah 55:7 // 76
Isaiah 55:8 // 53
Isaiah 64:6 // 35
Isaiah 65:2 // 87
Jeremiah 2:13 // 74
Jeremiah 10:2-16 // 221
Jeremiah 19:4 // 170
Jeremiah 23:5-6 // 155
Jeremiah 28:9 // 146
Jeremiah 31:31-34 // 38, 184
Ezekiel 16:21 // 170
Ezekiel 33:33 // 146
Daniel 7:13 // 166
Daniel 7:14 // 166
Hosea 11:1 // 176
Hosea 13:9 // 224
Jonah 4:11 // 170
Micah 4:2 // 166
Micah 5:2 // 166
Zephaniah 3:17 // 52
Zechariah 11:12-13 // 167
Malachi 2:16 // 226
Malachi 3:6 // 58
Malachi 4:5 // 39
Malachi 4:6 // 173
Matthew 1:1 // 173
Matthew 1:18-25 // 227
Matthew 1:21 // 41
Matthew 1:25 // 166
Matthew 1:6 // 155, 165
Matthew 2 // 171
Matthew 2:2 // 155
Matthew 2:13-15 // 167, 176
Matthew 2:26 // 166
Matthew 3 // 171
Matthew 3:1-3 // 155
Matthew 3:15 // 88
Matthew 3:17 // 166
Matthew 4:10-11 // 168, 172
Matthew 5:3-11 // 212
Matthew 5:21 // 164, 211
Matthew 5:22 // 211
Matthew 5:27 // 164, 211
Matthew 5:28 // 211
Matthew 5:33 // 164
Matthew 5:38 // 164
Matthew 5:43 // 164

Matthew 5:43-44 // 211
Matthew 7:13-14 // 45
Matthew 7:28-29 // 19
Matthew 9:15 // 225
Matthew 11:28 // 115, 126
Matthew 12-1-8 // 121
Matthew 12:18 // 166
Matthew 12:39 // 164, 165
Matthew 12:42 // 165
Matthew 12:49-50 // 197
Matthew 13:38 // 105
Matthew 14:13-21 // 150
Matthew 14:22-33 // 150
Matthew 16:18 // 165
Matthew 16:21 // 22
Matthew 18:3-5 // 171
Matthew 18:21-22 // 193
Matthew 19:26 // 53
Matthew 21:10 // 19
Matthew 21:37-38 // 166
Matthew 21:4-5 // 155
Matthew 22:1-11 // 230
Matthew 22:11-14 // 230
Matthew 22:37-39 // 211
Matthew 24:30-31 // 135
Matthew 24:31 // 228
Matthew 25:13 // 228
Matthew 25:31-34 // 157
Matthew 25:41 // 45
Matthew 25:41-46 // 158
Matthew 26:5-61 // 167
Matthew 26:15 // 167
Matthew 26:27-29 // 226
Matthew 26:28 // 102
Matthew 26:31 // 166
Matthew 26:38-45 // 172
Matthew 26:63-66 // 219
Matthew 26:64 // 102
Matthew 27:11 // 156
Matthew 27:37 // 156
Matthew 27:51 // 205
Matthew 28:19-20 // 179
Mark 1:15 // 29, 165
Mark 4:35-41 // 150
Mark 10:32-34 // 149
Mark 10:45 // 164
Mark 12:6-7 // 166
Mark 12:17 // 165
Mark 12:31 // 193
Mark 14:61 – 22
Luke 1:35 // 187

Luke 1:47 // 188
Luke 2:47 // 165
Luke 2:52 // 167
Luke 3:8 // 202
Luke 4:1 // 167
Luke 4:16-21 // 164
Luke 4:40 // 18
Luke 5:20 // 19
Luke 9:23-26 // 206
Luke 12:35-37 // 210
Luke 20:13-15 // 166
Luke 22:42 // 131
Luke 23:2-3 // 22
Luke 23:20-25 // 168
Luke 23:32 // 167
Luke 23:34 // 194
Luke 23:39 // 22
Luke 23:39- 22, 43 // 167
Luke 23:40-43 // 158
Luke 24:6 // 102
Luke 24:13-27 // 24
Luke 24:19 // 149, 165
John 1:1-2 // 167
John 1:1 // 173
John 1:1 // 219
John 1:4 // 138
John 1:5 // 138
John 1:10 // 167
John 1:10 // 75
John 1:14 // 136
John 1:14 // 97
John 1:29 // 42, 185, 204
John 1:51 // 180
John 2:19-22 // 150
John 2:22 // 188
John 3:14-15 // 87
John 3:16 // 59, 163, 188
John 3:2 // 167
John 3:20 // 56
John 4:7-14 // 74
John 5:23 // 166
John 5:39 // 30
John 5:46 // 163
John 6:20 // 218
John 6:25 // 217
John 6:30-31 // 81
John 6:32-35 // 82
John 6:35 // 100
John 6:46-51 // 83
John 7:3-5 // 166
John 7:37 // 75

John 7:37-38 // 137
John 7:37-39 // 217
John 7:41-44 // 137
John 8:12 // 99, 137, 217
John 8:24 // 217
John 8:24 // 231
John 8:28 // 217
John 8:31-32 // 164
John 8:44 // 105
John 8:59 // 218
John 8:59 // 219
John 10:11 // 166
John 10:28 // 226
John 10:7-9 // 98
John 10:9 // 62, 217
John 11:1-44 // 150
John 11:35 // 53
John 13:8 // 98
John 13:19 // 218
John 13:33 // 227
John 14:2-3 // 164, 227
John 14:6 // 13, 47, 205, 217, 231
John 15:11 // 140
John 15:18 // 57, 179
John 15:18-19 // 166
John 15:23-25 // 57
John 16:7 // 103
John 16:16 // 163
John 16:33 // 204
John 18:4-5 // 218
John 19:7 // 163
John 20:30-31 // 216
John 24:5 // 102
Acts 1:9 // 102
Acts 2:1-4 // 134
Acts 2:22-23
Acts 2:22-39 // 49
Acts 2:23 // 131
Acts 3:12-18 // 167
Acts 4:12 // 167
Acts 5:1-11 // 148
Acts 7:9 // 167
Acts 10:38 // 150, 167
Acts 13:23 // 167
Acts 20:7 // 126
Romans 1:7 // 152
Romans 1:18-21 // 118
Romans 2:5-11 // 57
Romans 2:5-8 // 53
Romans 2:14-16 // 116

Romans 2:20 // 53
Romans 3:24-25 // 101
Romans 4:1-8 // 120
Romans 5:10 // 56
Romans 5:10-11 // 104
Romans 5:12 // 168, 169
Romans 5:13-14 // 169
Romans 5:15-17 // 172
Romans 5:18-19 // 54
Romans 6:23 // 169
Romans 7:11 // 210
Romans 7:13 // 53
Romans 8:1 // 197
Romans 8:3 // 136
Romans 8:6-8 // 104
Romans 8:7-8 // 56
Romans 8:9-11 // 197
Romans 8:11 // 104
Romans 8:29-30 // 208
Romans 8:31-39 // 152
Romans 8:32 // 198
Romans 12:1 // 198
Romans 12:2 // 158
Romans 12:17-19 // 193
Romans 12:20-21 // 193
Romans 13:1-7 // 178
Romans 13:14 // 191
Romans 14:17 // 139
Romans 15:4 // 158
1 Corinthians 1:23 // 126
1 Corinthians 5:6-7 // 132
1 Corinthians 5:7 // 131
1 Corinthians 6:9-10 // 157
1 Corinthians 6:19 // 103
1 Corinthians 6:19-20 // 136, 198, 226
1 Corinthians 6:20 // 225
1 Corinthians 10:1-4 // 70
1 Corinthians 11:1 // 191
1 Corinthians 11:23-25 // 206
1 Corinthians 11:23-26 // 42
1 Corinthians 15 // 229
1 Corinthians 15:4 // 102
1 Corinthians 15:12-17 // 102
1 Corinthians 15:12-19 // 133
1 Corinthians 15:20 // 132
1 Corinthians 15:22 // 197
1 Corinthians 15:47 // 172

1 Corinthians 15:51-52 // 135

1 Corinthians 16:2 // 126

2 Corinthians 1:10 // 164

2 Corinthians 5:10 // 35

2 Corinthians 5:14-17 // 204

2 Corinthians 5:20 // 212

2 Corinthians 5:21 // 70, 88, 190

2 Corinthians 6:2 // 212

2 Corinthians 6:18 // 203

2 Corinthians 11:2 // 167, 225

2 Corinthians 12:9-11 – 197

Galatians 2:19-20 // 204

Galatians 2:20 // 192

Galatians 3:13-14 // 87

Galatians 3:16 // 65, 95

Galatians 3:24 // 95, 210

Galatians 3:27 // 191

Galatians 3:28 // 224

Galatians 4:4-5 // 29

Galatians 5:22-23 // 139

Galatians 5:25 // 203

Galatians 5:26 // 196

Galatians 6:17 // 202

Ephesians 1:3-14 // 103

Ephesians 1:3-6 225

Ephesians 1:13 // 202

Ephesians 1:13-14 // 227

Ephesians 2:1-3 // 203

Ephesians 2:2 // 203

Ephesians 2:3 // 203

Ephesians 2:4-8 // 167

Ephesians 2:5 // 203

Ephesians 2:8-9 // 119, 230

Ephesians 3:17 // 197

Ephesians 4:11 // 178

Ephesians 4:23-24 // 158

Ephesians 4:30 // 52

Ephesians 4:31 // 193

Ephesians 5 // 225

Ephesians 5:1 // 191

Ephesians 5:1-2 // 192

Ephesians 5:22-24 // 225

Ephesians 5:27 // 228

Ephesians 6:1 // 178

Philippians 2:5-8 // 187

Philippians 2:7 // 157

Philippians 2:7 // 167

Philippians 2:8-11 // 235

Philippians 2:9-11 // 168

Philippians 2:10 // 167

Philippians 4:13 // 196

Philippians 4:19 // 167, 198

Colossians 1:21 // 56

Colossians 1:21-22 // 104

Colossians 1:27 // 197

Colossians 2:13-14 // 151, 158

Colossians 2:16-17 // 30, 122, 129

Colossians 3:10 // 158

Colossians 3:1-14 // 192

1 Thessalonians 4:16 // 135, 228

1 Thessalonians 5:2-6 // 227

2 Thessalonians 1:5-7 // 192

2 Thessalonians 1:7-10 // 235

1 Timothy 2:4 // 230

1 Timothy 3:12 // 202

2 Timothy 3:12 // 204

Hebrews 1:3 // 102

Hebrews 4:14 // 162

Hebrews 4:17 // 162

Hebrews 4:9-10 // 124

Hebrews 6:17-20 // 180

Hebrews 7:22 // 162, 180

Hebrews 7:23-28 // 151

Hebrews 7:25 // 100, 158

Hebrews 7:26 // 101

Hebrews 7:3 // 162

Hebrews 8 // 107

Hebrews 8:7-13 // 125

Hebrews 9 // 109

Hebrews 9:1-5 // 98

Hebrews 9:11-15 // 43

Hebrews 9:13-14 // 158

Hebrews 9:15-28 // 102

Hebrews 10 // 111

Hebrews 10:1-10 // 96

Hebrews 10:10 // 101

Hebrews 10:11 // 101

Hebrews 10:11-14 // 102

Hebrews 10:12 // 102

Hebrews 10:19-20 // 100, 205

Hebrews 10:25 // 125

Hebrews 10:29-31 // 105

Hebrews 12:6 // 86

Hebrews 12:24 // 44, 162

Hebrews 13:11-12 // 136

Hebrews 13:12 // 163

James 1:17 // 58

James 1:2-4 // 140

James 4:4 // 57, 195

James 4:5-6 // 196

James 4:6-10 // 127

1 Peter 1:1-5 // 152

1 Peter 1:3-5 // 158

1 Peter 1:8-9 // 139

1 Peter 1:10-12 // 29

1 Peter 1:18-19 // 226

1 Peter 2:8 // 126

1 Peter 3:18-22 // 61

1 John 2:1-2 // 61

1 John 3:1 // 90

1 John 3:4 // 35

1 John 3:8 // 105

1 John 3:16 // 90

1 John 4:8 // 58, 166

1 John 4:9-10 // 90

1 John 4:10 // 61

1 John 5:11-12 // 167

2 John 7 // 188

Jude 3 // 194

Revelation 1:4-5 // 162

Revelation 2:17 // 203

Revelation 3:4 // 228

Revelation 3:19 // 86

Revelation 5:10 // 171

Revelation 5:11-14 // 44

Revelation 6:12-17 // 45

Revelation 19:8 // 228

Revelation 19:9 // 210

Revelation 19:11-16 // 156

Revelation 19:14 // 228

Revelation 19:16 // 165

Revelation 20:11-15 // 45

Revelation 21:1-4 // 229

Revelation 21:1-8 // 46

Revelation 21:3 // 136

Revelation 21:8 // 55

Revelation 21:21-27 // 47

Revelation 22:1-6 // 47

Revelation 22:3 // 173

Assembled by Jason Hilliard

Simplify the Basic Concepts.
Develop an Edge for Advanced Studies.

INTRO TO BIBLICAL GREEK Includes a weekly lesson schedule, student worksheets, quizzes, tests, and answer keys for one semester. Students will go beyond simple memorization and actually grasp the meaning and message of the Greek texts! 10th – 12th grade.

Intro to Biblical Greek PLP & *It's Not Greek To Me* DVD Package
$33.99 978-0-89051-818-2

It's Not Greek To Me DVD
$19.99 UPC: 713438102283

Intro to Biblical Greek PLP
$13.99 978-0-89051-817-5

Master Books®
A Division of New Leaf Publishing Group
www.masterbooks.net

Available where fine books are sold and nlpg.com.